STEP OR STUMBLE: THE OBAMA ADMINISTRATION'S PIVOT TO ASIA

HEARING

BEFORE THE

SUBCOMMITTEE ON ASIA AND THE PACIFIC

OF THE

COMMITTEE ON FOREIGN AFFAIRS
HOUSE OF REPRESENTATIVES

ONE HUNDRED FOURTEENTH CONGRESS

SECOND SESSION

DECEMBER 6, 2016

Serial No. 114–239

Printed for the use of the Committee on Foreign Affairs

Available via the World Wide Web: http://www.foreignaffairs.house.gov/ or
http://www.gpo.gov/fdsys/

U.S. GOVERNMENT PUBLISHING OFFICE

22–865PDF   WASHINGTON : 2017

For sale by the Superintendent of Documents, U.S. Government Publishing Office
Internet: bookstore.gpo.gov   Phone: toll free (866) 512–1800; DC area (202) 512–1800
Fax: (202) 512–2104   Mail: Stop IDCC, Washington, DC 20402–0001

COMMITTEE ON FOREIGN AFFAIRS

EDWARD R. ROYCE, California, *Chairman*

CHRISTOPHER H. SMITH, New Jersey
ILEANA ROS-LEHTINEN, Florida
DANA ROHRABACHER, California
STEVE CHABOT, Ohio
JOE WILSON, South Carolina
MICHAEL T. McCAUL, Texas
TED POE, Texas
MATT SALMON, Arizona
DARRELL E. ISSA, California
TOM MARINO, Pennsylvania
JEFF DUNCAN, South Carolina
MO BROOKS, Alabama
PAUL COOK, California
RANDY K. WEBER SR., Texas
SCOTT PERRY, Pennsylvania
RON DeSANTIS, Florida
MARK MEADOWS, North Carolina
TED S. YOHO, Florida
CURT CLAWSON, Florida
SCOTT DesJARLAIS, Tennessee
REID J. RIBBLE, Wisconsin
DAVID A. TROTT, Michigan
LEE M. ZELDIN, New York
DANIEL DONOVAN, New York

ELIOT L. ENGEL, New York
BRAD SHERMAN, California
GREGORY W. MEEKS, New York
ALBIO SIRES, New Jersey
GERALD E. CONNOLLY, Virginia
THEODORE E. DEUTCH, Florida
BRIAN HIGGINS, New York
KAREN BASS, California
WILLIAM KEATING, Massachusetts
DAVID CICILLINE, Rhode Island
ALAN GRAYSON, Florida
AMI BERA, California
ALAN S. LOWENTHAL, California
GRACE MENG, New York
LOIS FRANKEL, Florida
TULSI GABBARD, Hawaii
JOAQUIN CASTRO, Texas
ROBIN L. KELLY, Illinois
BRENDAN F. BOYLE, Pennsylvania

AMY PORTER, *Chief of Staff*   THOMAS SHEEHY, *Staff Director*
JASON STEINBAUM, *Democratic Staff Director*

————

SUBCOMMITTEE ON ASIA AND THE PACIFIC

MATT SALMON, Arizona *Chairman*

DANA ROHRABACHER, California
STEVE CHABOT, Ohio
TOM MARINO, Pennsylvania
JEFF DUNCAN, South Carolina
MO BROOKS, Alabama
SCOTT PERRY, Pennsylvania
SCOTT DesJARLAIS, Tennessee

BRAD SHERMAN, California
AMI BERA, California
TULSI GABBARD, Hawaii
ALAN S. LOWENTHAL, California
GERALD E. CONNOLLY, Virginia
GRACE MENG, New York

CONTENTS

STEP OR STUMBLE: THE OBAMA ADMINISTRATION'S PIVOT TO ASIA

TUESDAY, DECEMBER 6, 2016

House of Representatives,
Subcommittee on Asia and the Pacific,
Committee on Foreign Affairs,
Washington, DC.

The subcommittee met, pursuant to notice, at 2:00 p.m., in room 2172, Rayburn House Office Building, Hon. Matt Salmon (chairman of the subcommittee) presiding.

Mr. SALMON. Good afternoon. The committee will come to order. The written statements will be included in the official hearing record. And without objection, the hearing record will remain open for 5 calendar days to allow statements, questions and extraneous materials for the record, subject to the length limitation in the rules.

Today marks my final hearing as chairman of this important subcommittee. It is truly an honor to have served on this subcommittee with my fellow distinguished members. My time as chairman, focused on the world's most dynamic region, has been punctuated with memories of meeting countless dedicated policy and business professionals, insights that I will carry with me beyond my tenure here on the grave—here on the Hill. Did I say grave? And hopefully, leaving a lasting mark on our Nation's Asia policy.

As the United States undergoes a notable transition, I convene this hearing to review the current administration's policy toward Asia, and to determine what tangible accomplishments the United States has made. More importantly, we will also form suggestions for the new administration's policy toward Asia.

We have come to the end of an administration whose signature foreign policy initiative has been a rebalance to the Asia-Pacific. I have long championed enhancing our engagement with the Asia-Pacific and our friends and our allies in the region. They have welcomed the rebalance as a strengthening of our regional relationships. But after 8 years of enhancing U.S. efforts in Asia, serious challenges to U.S. interests persist, and some of them have even grown. Today, I note that our posture in Asia is not what we hoped for when the pivot was introduced.

The TPP. As we reflect on the outgoing Obama administration's efforts in Asia, the Trans-Pacific Partnership may be end up being the administration's most lasting failure. The administration chose to use this economic agreement as our strategic anchor in Asia and tried to market the deal at home by saying that it would allow us to write the rules for free trade. Now, the prospect of TPP ratification in the United States is effectively dead, and our closest Asian partners are questioning the endurance of our leadership in the region.

This debacle endangers U.S. prestige in Asia, and it didn't need to happen. The administration's own arguments implied that China is now in a position to write the rules. And our national reputation has taken a hit, because the administration tied it to TPP without first establishing a national consensus by addressing deep domestic concerns about the potential impact on our economic viability.

As the next administration considers its economic and trade ties with Asia, it may now be better to approach negotiations bilaterally, perhaps starting with Japan. If we begin the bilateral process with Japan, we may be able to add other modern economies in the dialog in a more feasible approach directed at a core group.

Without a concerted economic engagement with all parts of Asia, China will fill the void with its willingness to fund much-needed infrastructure without regard to intellectual property, labor and environmental standards. China has been, and will continue to be, a land of contradictions, of challenges and opportunities. The need to strike a proper balance of working together on economic prosperity, with a willingness to stand firm when necessary, will continue under our President-elect's tenure.

Our business community and economy are under threat from regulations and policies designed to favor Chinese interests and domestic champions. Threats from cyber-enabled economic espionage and intellectual property theft continue unabated. The current administration has been more willing to make concessions and seems fearful of provoking China. I have been alarmed to witness the escalation of infringement on Hong Kong's self-governance and basic law with little to no U.S. pushback. Many in Congress have been similarly unsatisfied with the administration's halfhearted efforts to address Chinese human rights abuses and regional aggression, particularly with respect to the South China Sea.

Our regional allies and friends continue to call for further U.S. engagement and assistance. And it is my expectation that the next administration will seek to provide substantive reassurance to the region.

Taiwan. A lot of hoopla about Taiwan in the last few days. China has also been increasingly unreasonable toward Taiwan, which is in a more precarious position than ever. I was able to attend Tsai Ing-wen's swearing in. That was the third president of Taiwan that I have been able to attend the swearing in. I attended Lee Teng-hui's, the first truly elected president of Taiwan. I then attended Chen Shui-bian's, and I was able to be at Tsai Ing-wen's, much over the objections of some of the folks here. I was, I think, was the highest ranking Member of the Congress to—actually, I think I was the only Member of the Congress that I attended. After completing yet another successful democratic transition, Taiwan continues to prove that a free flourishing economically successful Chinese democracy in civil society is possible.

The surprise over President-elect Trump accepting a call from President Tsai Ing-wen has been an unnecessary distraction. The fact is, we are economically and militarily engaged with Taiwan as directed by the 1971 Taiwan Relations Act, and a phone call between principals should not garner such outrage.

I am further dismayed that the same Washington elites and press corps that hailed President Obama a hero for meeting with Iran's President Rouhani, a key supporter of terrorism across the globe, would become so distraught over a phone call. I fully expect that President-elect Trump and President Tsai will have a productive relationship that benefits both of our economies.

North Korea will continue to be a challenge that we must face head on. This has been one of the ultimate blunders of the Obama administration in Asia, the so-called strategic patience approach to North Korea. While Kim Jong Un has conducted increasingly powerful nuclear and ballistic missile tests, we have not seen anything that could be described as a strategy. If the past gives any indication of what to expect, North Korea could soon conduct another substantial provocation to welcome the U.S. President to office. Congress has been vigilant about applying pressure on the DPRK, and I anticipate that it will continue to look forward to new levers to stop North Korea's belligerent and dangerous behavior. Sanctions efforts led by Chairman Ed Royce have helped squeeze the DPRK from vital funding sources. Still, more can and has to be done, such as further cooperation and intelligence sharing between our allies, the Republic of Korea and Japan.

In addition, more can be done to increase the flow of information into North Korea. We can do much more to assist the people of North Korea to understand the truth of their reality. North Korea and provocation should always be met with resistance, and I look forward to a new strategy on this front.

This year, the administration's relationship with a long-time ally, the Philippines, fell apart. Newly elected President Duterte came out strongly in opposition of the United States. He has appeared to use the media to pit the United States against China, in an effort to renegotiate the long-standing alliance structure. Despite the trend of late, I am heartened to see that the Philippines President, and President-elect Trump, have shown each other mutual respect. And I am hopeful that this pivotal alliance will be rekindled from the top down and remain the force for good that it can be.

India. The administration halfheartedly sought to include India in the pivot, but the deep well of potential in our bilateral ties remains untapped. India struggles with infrastructure challenges, energy issues and difficult neighbors, but the two world's largest democracies are natural partners. There is a strong appetite within the United States to encourage India to take a stronger leadership role within the region. Leadership does come with responsibilities. As India seeks to garner closer commercial and defense relations with the U.S., it must take steps toward important reforms that will lay the foundation for increased ties.

I am skeptical that our interests in Asia have been substantially advanced over the last 8 years. The outgoing administration spoke often of intentions to refocus its efforts in Asia, but left nearly everything undone. Its landmark trade deal has failed. Being patient with North Korea has made us less secure. We have lost footing with a longtime ally in the Philippines, and our security guarantees throughout the region have been called into question by destabilizing actors. Looking ahead, I am very optimistic that the new administration, along with what I hope will be a unified Congress, can rebuild efforts in Asia, provide for a robust regional security, and promote lasting U.S. prosperity.

I am going to turn to the gentleman from California, Mr. Bera, to see if he would like to make an opening comment or two.

Mr. BERA. Certainly. Mr. Chairman, I would like to take this opportunity to thank you for your work over these last 2 years. Your leadership, your understanding of the region, your fluency in the Chinese language has been great. It has been a pleasure to travel to India, to China and to Taiwan with you. So we are going to miss that expertise and we are going to miss that leadership, and it really has been a pleasure for this Member of Congress serving with you, and I look forward to—hopefully, you will stay engaged in the region if opportunities present themselves to continue to stay engaged, but the best of luck in the future, and I do hope to continue working with you in that.

I will leave my further statements for the hearing. So thank you.

Mr. SALMON. I thank the gentleman. I recognize the other gentleman from California, Mr. Rohrabacher.

Mr. ROHRABACHER. Thank you very much, Mr. Chairman. Let me just note what an honor and pleasure it has been to work with you as friends and colleagues and patriots, trying to do what is best for our country and just—you will be missed and we hope that things go well. Let me just say we all are here for a short period of time. Our goal is—hopefully our goal has been to help make things better for the United States of America. Some people think our goal is to focus on making it a better world. That certainly is something positive, and that is, frankly, perceptions of what is good for the whole world is not necessarily what is good for the United States of America.

And we even have a new President who has made it very clear that that will be his criteria, what is good for the people of the United States of America. In that regard, I would suggest that in your area, you have so ably overseen in these last few years, that I would give the administration a D, I wouldn't give them an F, I would give them a D. And as the chairman just noted, what is going on with actions and hostile posturing and belligerency on the part of China has increased. North Korea's threatening behavior, as well as its actual arrogance, in dealing with the issue of nuclear weapons. Again, much more threatening than it was. And then we have the crumbling of our long-term relationships with Malaysia and with the Philippines. This, overall then, this pivot to Asia, that has been—in and of itself, has been a failure, but overall, I give the administration a D. And looking forward to hopefully next year, even on the other side of the aisle if they want to give it a rank, then maybe we will have an A. Let's see if we can all work for that.

Mr. SALMON. The chair recognizes the former chairman the subcommittee, Mr. Chabot.

Mr. CHABOT. Thank you very much, Mr. Chairman. I want to begin, again, by some of my colleagues who said thanking you for your years of service to this House, and especially for your stewardship of this committee. And I know that you know you had big shoes to fill when stepping into this role, they were mine. But you handled it very, very well, and have done a great job as chair of this committee. So I want to thank you for that. And we wish you the best of luck. I am sure you are going to be very successful in whatever it is. Have you decided yet? Or are you going to make an announcement here today?

Mr. SALMON. I don't know, I was going to try to be Secretary General of the U.N. What do you think?

Mr. CHABOT. Would you want that job?

Mr. SALMON. Not on your life.

Mr. ROHRABACHER. See what we can do.

Mr. CHABOT. Secretary of State Rohrabacher. But in any event, the pivot, to get to the topic at hand here, I think it has been one of the most frequently and poorly defined phrases of the Obama administration. Some experts have argued that it has been little more than an empty slogan. I hate to say that I tend to agree with that. The pivot has really been a sorry excuse for strategy. It has merely been a hodgepodge of contradictory ideas that is, without question, signaled indecision and weakness to challengers from Beijing to Pyongyang to Moscow.

The past several years have been especially disconcerting, particularly the administration's handling of China's growing assertiveness from building islands to now militarizing them. We failed to effectively stand up for our allies in the region, such as Taiwan. And I have to say, although I know some folks have been concerned about that, upset about that, I say more power to him for having taken that call. And Chinese bullying has to stop, and it has gotten worse and worse in recent years, and I think this administration has done little to push back on that. And I don't think you reward bad behavior, and I think that is what has been happening. Beijing's behavior has been more and more reprehensible, and it has been not nearly enough pushback.

And as I am sure all my colleagues believe, you know, we don't want to see any sort of military action in that part of the region. But as Ronald Reagan believed, it is through strength that you continue with the peace. Weakness invites military action in war, and I think that is what is happening now. And so I commend President-elect Trump for taking that call. I look forward to hearing the witnesses' testimony this afternoon, and I yield back.

Mr. SALMON. Thank you. Did any of the other committee members wish to make an opening statement? If not, then we go to the panel, we are really thankful to be joined today by Dr. Richard Ellings, president of the National Bureau of Asian Research. Great to see you again.

How is your wound from your baseball tournament? Are you doing better?

Mr. ELLINGS. Broken thumb, but I'm here.

Mr. SALMON. Well, I am glad to see you.

Dr. Derek Scissors, resident scholar——

Mr. ELLINGS. Too much information.

Mr. SCISSORS. I have no injuries.

Mr. SALMON. No injuries? Good. I don't think you would tell us if you did.

Ms. Kelley Currie, senior fellow at Project 2049

Institute. Great to see you again. And Mr. Barry Lynn, director of New America's Open Markets Program. We thank the panel for joining us today to share their experience and expertise.

And I am going to start with you, Dr. Ellings. Would you go ahead and turn your microphone on. And you all know the drill? When it turns amber, it is time to wrap up. I think you have about a minute to wrap up. I don't have a heavy gavel, but we don't have the power of the filibuster over here in the House, so you can't go on forever, so that is the drill. Thank you.

Go ahead Dr. Ellings.

STATEMENT OF RICHARD J. ELLINGS, PH.D., PRESIDENT, THE NATIONAL BUREAU OF ASIAN RESEARCH

Mr. ELLINGS. Chairman Salmon, Congressman Bera, when he gets here, Ranking Member Sherman and other extraordinarily distinguished members of the committee, it is an honor to share of my personal observations and views that are outlined in my written testimony. I plan to get through them quickly before they become obsolete. You know, there might be a Tweet. The pivot, better called the rebalance, has been a policy that might be termed enhanced more of the same.

I will make two contextual points, then assess the policy and conclude by suggesting some concrete things Congress can do working with the new administration.

First contextual point. For many reasons, this period of history appears to be a hinge moment, as someone put it recently. It is akin in too many ways to the years immediately preceding World Wars I and II, highlighted by the industrialization and rise of dissatisfied nationalistic authoritarian powers. And yet, it differs from these eras in noteworthy ways as well.

The nuances of this century's principle rising power, China. The proliferation of nuclear weapons and America's strategic engagement. The remarkable rise, power and ambitions of China comprise the central issue. As China watchers like to point out, the country has made enormous progress, but has all kinds of horrible problems. Its chief problem is that its unelected leadership under Xi Jinping is insecure and resorting to tighter control, repressive measures, and nationalistic appeals to bolster its popularity, capitalizing on historic grievances.

Correspondingly as foreign policies have become more aggressive, and at the same time, remain carefully calculated and, frankly, farsighted. China has a grand strategy to maximize its wealth, space and global influence, and to marginalize its most serious competitors, most notably, the United States. It has an eye for weak spots.

For many years, specialists have been predicting political crisis, or change, in China, they have been wrong. And yet, they are right about the future. But we have no ability now to protect when change will happen, or what kind of change.

Second contextual point. Viewed from a global perspective, power, no matter how the measure it, is concentrated heavily in the Asia-Pacific. I characterize the balance in the region as skewed multipolarity. It is skewed, in part, because China has led a one-sided arms buildup.

Given the uneven dispersion of power, the extraordinary pace of change in the balance of power, uncertainty in key countries, and increasing questions about U.S. leadership, ambiguity also describes the strategic environment. Ambiguity is not good. When nations have a difficult time understanding their strategic environment, many feel insecure and like to expand their allies and defenses. Some nations see opportunities to pursue ambitions.

In times like ours, nations are more prone to making calculations that lead to conflict. Our capacity to remain strong and committed, to exploit weaknesses in our competitors, and to form and sustain effective coalitions, will be the test of our leadership.

A quick assessment of the pivot. The intention to place greater policy focus on the Asia-Pacific is great. It is terrific, imperative, and goes back decades to the Clinton through George W. Bush administrations.

President Barack Obama's high profile pivot in fall of 2011 aimed to strengthen our alliances and friendships, engage China, bolster regional multiple lateral institutions, expand trade and investment, add to our military presence, at least, implicitly, in North Korea's nuclear program, advance democracy and human rights, a pact, and familiar agenda. But announced at full volume and short on specifics.

After 5 years, it is fair to judge the policy. Notwithstanding, a senior State Department official's recent statement that, and I quote, ''We're handing the next administration a success story in Asia.'' Seriously, that was said. ''The pivot and the predecessor policies on balance have failed to prepare us for the challenges of today, let alone tomorrow.''

We have not been operating from understanding of the world as it actually exists. We have failed repeatedly to understand and anticipate Russian intentions and policy, North Korean intentions and policy, and most importantly, Chinese intentions and policy. Furthermore, I see no evidence that we have contemplated strategies to avoid facing some type of Sino-Russian or Sino-Russian-North Korean-Pakistani coalition if, for example, hostilities were to break out in the Korean peninsula and in south Asia.

We are being compelled to position our world-leading military forces farther and farther off the Asian coastline. We have not come up with an effective answer to China's island-based building in the South China Sea. We have failed to prevent North Korea from achieving nuclear breakout.

Sequestration has prevented us from investing in many of the systems we will need to deter—if deterrence fails, to win—a future conflict in the region. In fact, we do not have a military strategy for the Asia-Pacific. We continue to treat trade with China as normal when the country is persistently mercantilists. U.S. companies are increasingly twisted into pretzels trying to operate in a market that is now the size of America's. Companies try to avoid upsetting the regime. They try to protect their IP unsuccessfully, and they compete with increasingly strong Chinese companies that are favored in myriad and mostly opaque ways.

Our regional leadership is weaker in part due to the apparent demise in the pivot's economic centerpiece, the Trans-Pacific Partnership. According to a smug daily, China daily article published days ago with regard to trade ''China's happy to write the rules with all its partners.''

Any further faltering of our commitment to rebalancing would jeopardize, just to name one important example, our strategic relationship with India. The hope for a political liberalization of China has not developed from its accession to the World Trade Organization, or from the world otherwise engaging China. Indeed, by most measures, the regime is less liberal, more repressive today than any time since it joined the WTO. I would like to go when it is possible, when you think it is reasonable through a number of specific suggestions that answer each one of these issues.

[The prepared statement of Mr. Ellings follows:]

NBR THE NATIONAL BUREAU of ASIAN RESEARCH

Testimony before the House Committee on Foreign Affairs
Subcommittee on Asia and the Pacific

United States House of Representatives

Hearing:

"Step or Stumble: The Obama Administration's Pivot to Asia"

Testimony by:
Richard J. Ellings
President
The National Bureau of Asian Research

December 6, 2016
2172 Rayburn House Office Building

Seattle and Washington, D.C.

1819 L STREET NW, NINTH FLOOR ~ WASHINGTON, D.C. 20036 USA ~ PHONE 202-547-0707, FAX 202-547-0700 ~ NBRDC@NBR.ORG, WWW.NBR.ORG

The National Bureau of Asian Research

Congressional Testimony
(December 2016)

Chairman Salmon, Ranking member Sherman, distinguished members of the Committee,

It is an honor to share my observations and views with you this afternoon, views that are my own, not those of The National Bureau of Asian Research (NBR). NBR is Senator Henry M. "Scoop" Jackson's dream and legacy, and all of us associated with NBR strive to ensure that that legacy is bipartisan, informed by history and the highest-quality research, and focused on the essential interests of the United States.

The "pivot," better called the rebalance, has been a policy of what might be termed "enhanced more of the same." Let me address the policy first by making two contextual points, and then by assessing recent developments as they relate to the pivot. I will conclude by suggesting some alternative, concrete things that Congress can do in working with the new administration.

First contextual point: Where are we in history? For many reasons this period now appears to be a "hinge moment," as someone wrote recently. It's akin in too many ways to the years immediately preceding World Wars I and II, highlighted by the industrialization and rise of dissatisfied, nationalistic, authoritarian powers. And it differs from these eras in noteworthy ways as well: nuances of the principal rising power, China; the proliferation of nuclear weapons; and America's strategic engagement.

China is the central issue. Today, as this committee's members understand, this continental-sized, dissatisfied, nationalistic, authoritarian power continues to rise, albeit more slowly than it did in the preceding three and a half decades. It continues to industrialize, broaden its services sector, and gain power according to most hard measures. Its industrial sector is at least one and a half times the size of

The National Bureau of Asian Research   *Congressional Testimony*
(December 2016)

America's, and in many ways this sector is more integrated vertically as well as horizontally than ours. Often these days we are the assemblers. China has replaced Russia as the number-two military power in the world.

Nonetheless, as China watchers like to point out, the country has all kinds of problems, from environmental degradation and demographic issues to corruption and weak rule of law. Its chief problem is that its unelected leadership is insecure and resorting to tighter control, repressive measures, and nationalistic appeals to bolster its popularity, capitalizing on historical grievances. Correspondingly, its foreign policies have become more aggressive in recent years, far-reaching, and, frankly, farsighted. China has a grand strategy to maximize its wealth, space, and influence and to marginalize its most serious competitors, most notably the United States. Its economic policies have been more, not less, mercantilist in recent years. America's and others' intellectual property (IP) seems to be targeted as much today as ever. Meanwhile, China continues to not help in dealing with Pyongyang, to pursue its extraordinary military modernization, to expand its reach in the South China Sea, and to engage in military harassment of Japan.

Although led by a communist party and driven by extraordinary ambition, and notwithstanding its building bases on islets in the South China Sea, China does not evince a tendency toward direct aggression and conquest of the type witnessed in the mid-twentieth century. It has launched an ambitious set of nationalist, not ideological, programs to bolster its wealth, influence, and prestige globally through the One Belt, One Road initiative, Asian Infrastructure Investment Bank, and Regional Comprehensive Economic Partnership.

But China does pose the challenge of potentially dominating Asia with many values that conflict with those of the post–World War II order. If I were to speculate about what a China-led regional or world order would look like, I would extend what Chinese policies and politics look like today. China would aim to lead a suzerain international system, in which

The National Bureau of Asian Research

Congressional Testimony
(December 2016)

its national leadership would continue to be a melded political, business, and military leadership. A form of China-led mercantilism would count for the international economy, as China shows little evidence of trusting markets for what it deems important products and services such as energy and banking. The resulting system would be fragile because China itself would most likely continue to be led by an insecure, unelected, inherently corrupt elite, and states would not be treated as equals. An insecure Chinese leadership would certainly not tolerate anything close to a peer competitor, especially in Asia. The world would not likely be as prosperous, open, and law-based as it is today. It might be trifurcated into competing North American, European, and Asian centers of power.

For many years, specialists have been predicting political change in China to match its economic achievements. They have been wrong to date, and yet they are right about the future. But we have <u>no</u> ability now to predict <u>when</u> change will actually transpire, or what <u>kind</u> of change. Hope for change cannot be the basis for U.S. policy.

Second contextual point: Viewed from a global, systemic perspective, power is concentrating overwhelmingly in the Asia-Pacific, where all of the world's principal military powers and several of the key middle powers pursue their competing as well as shared national interests. (These countries, in rough descending order of military power, are the United States, China, Russia, India, Japan, South Korea, Pakistan, and North Korea.) Six of these eight powers possess nuclear weapons, and the other two are near nuclear. One, the United States, can project conventional power globally. One, China, is seeking that capability, at least regionally. I characterize the balance in the region as *skewed multipolarity*. It is skewed in part because China has pursued a one-sided arms build-up. For example, whereas China's military budget has increased twelvefold in the past 27 years, Japan's is virtually unchanged in this period.

The National Bureau of Asian Research　　　　　　　　*Congressional Testimony*
(December 2016)

Given the uneven dispersion of power, the extraordinary pace of change in the balance of power, changes in the domestic affairs of key countries, and increasing questions about U.S. leadership that are voiced in the region, *ambiguity* also describes today's strategic environment. Ambiguity is not good. When nations have a difficult time understanding their strategic environments, many feel insecure and look to expand their allies and defenses; some nations see opportunities to pursue ambitions. China and Russia have been perceiving opportunities, and acting accordingly, to expand their influence and undermine and even replace global and regional institutions—Russia by outright conquest, China by somewhat more subtle and certainly more clever means.

Today's remarkable economic interdependence, reminding one of pre–World War I conditions, cannot obscure these salient realities. In times like ours, nations are more prone to making calculations that lead to conflict. There is less margin for error by policymakers.

A quick assessment of the pivot: Multiple administrations have pursued a fairly consistent set of U.S. policies that have sustained general peace and made for an economic miracle in the region but not been adjusted to address the tremendous challenges gathering. While terribly named, the pivot is, in fact, an old and exceedingly helpful concept. The intention to place greater policy focus on the Asia-Pacific goes back decades to the Clinton administration and was emphasized at the outset of President George W. Bush's first term, which aimed primarily at bolstering relationships with allies and friends combined with regional trade liberalization.

President Barack Obama aimed more broadly in the "pivot" in fall 2011, to strengthen our alliances and friendships, further engage China, bolster regional multilateral institutions, expand trade and investment, strengthen our military presence, end North Korea's nuclear program, and advance democracy and human rights—all to enhance peace, prosperity, and democracy in the region. However, notwithstanding a top State Department official's recent statement that "we are handing the next administration a success story in Asia," the pivot and its predecessor policies on balance have failed to prepare us for the challenges of today and tomorrow.

a) We have not been operating from a strategic assessment of our core, defendable interests in the world and of the directions in which key players are moving. We have failed again and again to understand and anticipate Russian intentions and policy, North Korean intentions and policy, and most importantly Chinese intentions and policy. I see no evidence that we have undertaken a serious assessment of the kinds of coalitions that we may face should international tensions rise further and polarization take place. Have we contemplated facing some type of Sino-Russian or Sino-Russian-North Korean-Pakistani coalition if, for example, hostilities were to break out on the Korean Peninsula, in the Taiwan Strait, or in the Sea of Japan? I see no peacetime U.S. strategy built on a tough-minded global assessment—a strategy that, if pursued, might reduce the chances of our facing such coalitions and help contain any hostilities to the commons.

b) We continue to treat trade with China as normal, when what we are facing is a strategic-industrial Chinese policy of extraordinary scope and impact, including impeding our ability to capitalize on our innovations and to innovate in the first place.

c) U.S. companies are increasingly twisted into pretzels trying to operate in China and to access a market that is now about the size of America's. Companies remain under pressure to avoid getting on the bad side of the regime; they try to protect their IP unsuccessfully; and they compete with increasingly strong local companies that are favored in myriad ways. The situation for our companies is tougher, not better.

d) The hoped-for political liberalization of China has not developed
   from its accession to the World Trade Organization (WTO) or from
   the world otherwise engaging China. In fact, by most measures the
   regime is less liberal today than at any time since it joined the WTO.

e) Sequestration and "business as usual" procurement have hampered
   our efforts to do the serious work needed to deter—and if deterrence
   fails, be prepared to win—a conflict in the region.

f) In fact, we do not have a military strategy for the Asia-Pacific. We
   have not decided how to respond to China's "gray aggression," island
   building in the South China Sea or harassment of the Senkaku Islands
   by Chinese government-directed fishing boats and the Chinese Coast
   Guard. We have not decided what is essential to us or what winning
   would be for various contingencies. Is the effective control of the
   South China Sea by China crossing a red line or not? Have we
   adequately prepared, should war be thrust upon us, for a conventional
   arms victory fought over the commons? What are the red lines for our
   responding militarily in the commons?

g) Indeed, China and North Korea pose expansive and far greater, not
   smaller, challenges to the United States and its allies than before the
   pivot. To deter or defeat Chinese forces currently, we are being
   forced to position our forces farther and farther off the Chinese
   coastline. We have failed to prevent North Korea from achieving
   nuclear breakout.

h) Our leadership in the region is also weaker due to the apparent demise
   of the Trans-Pacific Partnership (TPP). According to a smug *China
   Daily* article published days ago, with regard to trade "China is happy
   to write the rules with all its partners," meaning China's partners in
   its Regional Comprehensive Economic Partnership initiative.

i) Any further faltering of our commitment to "rebalancing" would jeopardize, just to name one important example, our growing strategic relationship with India.

j) Regarding China's domestic situation, we have not responded substantively to Xi Jinping's so-called anti-corruption campaign and other polices creating the most repressive conditions in China in decades. We have not reacted substantively to China's increasingly bold moves to silence critics outside its borders, including its kidnapping, coercion, and trying of foreign nationals. Our passivity risks conveying the impression that we no longer believe that we hold the moral high ground or care about human rights, or, worse, that we are now intimidated by China's wealth and power.

Given this assessment of current policy, you might not be surprised that I think that we ought to do some things differently. In my view, time is of the essence. We do not have the luxury now of letting our own politics extend beyond the water's edge, nor pursuing a strategy that is "enhanced more of the same."

a) End using the term "pivot," but indeed pay more attention to the Asia-Pacific because the region is where power is concentrated, the threat of really big war looms largest, and the global economy is now centered. I'm fine with calling it the Asia-Indo-Pacific, but I don't because it's awkward to say.

b) End sequestration and require a reassessment of U.S. strategic interests, challenges, and opportunities globally and for the Asia-Pacific.

c) Pay considerable attention to our allies and friends, including India, and not just verbally or during your and the administration's personal visits to Asia. In general, we will be more successful in Asia by speaking more softly in public on strategic issues, while without fanfare rebuilding our credibility with meaningful investments, coordination, and actions. Verbal humiliation is less effective than firm policy.

d) Relaunch the TPP or a substitute as soon as possible so that the United States regains the high ground in regional leadership.

e) At the same time. Congress needs to ensure that the TPP or its substitute allows for national punitive responses to international IP theft and against predatory foreign industrial policies.

f) Treat China in a truthful and business-like manner. The president needs to utilize the powers granted in Section 1637 of the 2015 National Defense Authorization Act to retaliate against foreign entities that steal American IP, including Chinese entities, and to report to Congress on the issue as this law requires. My hunch is that the scale of IP theft will decline precipitously as we ratchet up a firm response.

g) The Committee on Foreign Investment in the United States needs beefing up and standards revised. The tangled web of Chinese strategic policies and companies poses a large and complex set of business and national security challenges.

h) Once we complete our assessment of the international strategic environment, we need to decide on core interests and goals consonant with U.S. power. It would be preferable, it seems to me, to be prepared to win unambiguously and with our allies a conventional fight in the commons (thus enhancing deterrence) as opposed to having only the capacity to win a war requiring less credible direct strikes on China and risking reciprocal strikes against the U.S. homeland, strikes that could turn nuclear quickly.

i) Accordingly, we need to make some fundamental decisions about how we will counter China's rapidly evolving capabilities and the challenges they present to U.S. assured access. Decisions about strategies and concepts of operation will be necessary if we are to make sensible decisions about R&D and procurement, among other issues. It is urgent that we decide what we need: Do we need more nuclear submarines, new long-range bombers, new generations of cruise missiles, or larger numbers of unmanned aerial vehicles and unmanned underwater vehicles?

j) Burden-sharing is imbedded into our close alliance relationships in Asia. As part of our reassessment of the strategic environment and the requirements that emerge from that assessment, cost items for further support from our allies should be identified and negotiated prudently.

k) China's interests today include supporting North Korea as a buffer, as a serious distraction for us requiring significant attention and resources, and as a potential front if hostilities break out between China and the United States. Terminal High Altitude Area Defense (THAAD) and other deployments that we deem strategically imperative must go forward. With an appropriate level of deployments, China may recalculate its support of a nuclear North Korea.

l) A word about Taiwan. The People's Republic of China has long defined a core interest to be the peaceful reunification of Taiwan and that Taiwan is a part of China, and we agreed to these stipulations with normalization of relations. We also committed ourselves to ensuring the integrity of Taiwan so that the reunification process is, in fact, peaceful, which is all the more important now due to Taiwan's remarkable democracy and the model that democracy provides. A congratulatory call from a democratically elected Taiwanese president to the U.S. president elect may not fit the habit of past presidents-elect, but it need not disrupt positive relations going forward. The Chinese leadership has a strong interest ahead in working with President Trump on a host of issues, and my guess is that this phone call by itself does

The National Bureau of Asian Research   *Congressional Testimony*
(December 2016)

not preclude—and may even enhance—constructive relations ahead.

m) Human rights policies underscore our claim to moral leadership. For this reason, and as an antidote to the anti-U.S., anti-Japan, and anti-Western propaganda coming out of Beijing incessantly, I would urge chronicling meticulously and publicizing methodically human rights violations, including international kidnappings, and their political origins. We need policies that make clear the superiority of freedom-loving nations based upon rule of law and limited, democratic government.

In summary, there is no acceptable alternative to U.S. leadership in the Asia-Pacific. No less than in Europe, we cannot allow one country, let alone a dissatisfied, nationalistic, authoritarian one, to dominate the region. That doesn't mean war is inevitable. A peaceful order in the Asia-Pacific that protects core U.S. interests and values is sustainable, but it will require our commitment, a new strategy, and exceedingly deft and intelligent leadership. While this is not a repeat of the simpler Cold War, the stakes are global, as the United States' failure at the center of world power would undercut our credibility elsewhere, including in Europe and the Middle East.

Mr. SALMON. Thank you very much, Dr. Ellings. Dr. Scissors, thank you. I understand this is your second time testifying before the panel. Thank you for not letting us not scare you off from the first time. We are really thrilled to you have you here again.

STATEMENT OF DEREK M. SCISSORS, PH.D., RESIDENT SCHOLAR, AMERICAN ENTERPRISE INSTITUTE

Mr. SCISSORS. Thank you, Mr. Chairman. I enjoyed the first time, and hope I will enjoy the second time. Thank you to the committee for having me a second time.

My remarks are going to be restricted to economics, which is, of course, important in our engagement in the region, but is only a partial view. I want to state that at the outset.

On the economic view, the next administration, the Trump administration, can do much better than the Obama administration did. However, that isn't going to be easy. We are caught between, on one hand, a China that is engaged in predatory trade that harms the United States, and American commitments to open markets and competition that help the United States. And while there is plenty of scope for U.S. improvement, that does not mean we will be able to carry it out. So I will try to address the future more than the past.

In terms of addressing the past, the Trans-Pacific Partnership is the obvious issue on the economic side. I have an odd view in America today which is, I didn't like the treaty because it didn't liberalize enough, not because it was too radical and too pro market.

I was at the Heritage Foundation for 5 years and at that time, I wrote multiple pieces praising the idea of the Trans-Pacific Partnership and praising the Obama administration for initiating it. I thought it was a great idea.

When I saw the text in November of last year, I changed my mind, because I actually read the agreement, which a lot of people don't do, if I might say under my breath. Oh, there is a microphone. I'm sorry. It did not create the opportunities for American workers that all of us at Democrat, Republican, conservative, liberal we want, and in particular, the U.S. is the most comprehensive services exporter in the world, and there are too many exceptions in liberalizing services trade. And as a result, I, the International Trade Commission, others, do not see gains for the U.S. from services liberalization in the Trans-Pacific Partnership.

I won't spend a lot of time. The point is, the TPP doesn't do what we need it to do economically. That is why President Obama began to start talking about writing the rules instead of economic benefits. He started talking about the diplomatic case for TPP. Those are all true. But the number one role of a trade agreement is to bring economic benefits through trade, and the TPP does not do that. So I will not be sorry to see it go. That is one point.

Turning in the other direction, something that I am worried about, I have written about, I wrote in my written testimony, I don't want the United States to swing all the way to the side of being protectionists. The Trump campaign cited a think tank that represents the labor movement, talking about how the trade deficits costs U.S. jobs. That is not true. We ran trade surpluses during the Depression, it did not help us on the job front.

Our trade deficit plunged in 2009, it did it not help us on the job front. Logically when we are rich, we buy more in the way of imports, and when we are poor, we don't. If you force the trade deficit down, and my colleagues may talk about this, you are going to hurt America's rivals. It is true. You are also going to hurt America's friends and allies, because we trade with them and they are involved in supply chains. You are going to damage the global economic system.

So I am going to talk in a second about sanctions against China, because I think there are some that are necessary. I don't want us to go too far to become a protectionist country, where we think trade balance is good economic goal, because it isn't.

Let's talk about sanctions in China. We can label China a currency manipulator; it is a currency manipulator, so it is a good label. It won't actually bring back U.S. jobs, because when you try to connect China's currency value to U.S. jobs, you don't get a connection.

Where we know the Chinese are harming us is blocking our exports. When Americans get cheap imports, at least we get a benefit from buying the cheap imports. It helps our consumers.

When a Chinese or other countries block our exports, there is nothing for us but cost. And China does that. It is the largest trading country in the world, so it is more important when China does it, when Bolivia does it, for example. And they protect their state-owned enterprises from competition, and that is a serious barrier to U.S. exports, in particular, U.S. services exports.

Reciprocity is a legitimate idea and a response. We shouldn't be narrow minded about it, we shouldn't be protectionist about it, but we should say, you are going to block our trade, we don't have an obligation to allow all your trade to occur.

Another issue that we are all familiar with is IP theft. China the biggest stealer of intellectual property in the world. Tens of millions of Americans have jobs supported by intellectual property; it is not just about high-technology, it is about any innovation. We need to act against companies that have stolen or—that have received stolen intellectual property, not just the thieves which the Obama administration did in a small way, but the companies that have benefited and compete against American companies because they have taken stolen intellectual property from whoever who stole it. That is a sanction that needs to go forward.

Something that I know you all have been discussing, and will be discussed in the next Congress, is the Committee on Foreign Investment in the United States, Chinese investment in the United States generally is beneficial, but there are some sectors where we do not want Chinese investment. And so, you know, without getting into the CFIUS debate, I would say that assigning more resources to reviewing investment is a benefit for the United States, both economically and in terms of national security.

I am already being warned, but I do want to talk a little bit about positive steps, not just sanctions against China. I would welcome the phone call, but I welcome it for a particular reason, I think the U.S. could side a FTA with Taiwan. During this administration, I think that would be a good idea.

Japan, as the chairman mentioned, is a superb goal, much more complicated, much more difficult, harder politically. Taiwan is 23 million people, they are not going to steal American jobs, so we have an advantage in talking to Taiwan.

There are countries, India, Indonesia, Philippines Vietnam, these are very rapid growth countries. I would not call for FTAs for these countries, they aren't ready, and we aren't ready. But trying to improve trade relations with these countries would bring economic benefits to the United States; there the important countries in the region to focus on economically.

My last point before I stop, we don't normally think of corporate tax reform as bearing on the Asia-Pacific, but in this case, there are plans in the works that have border tax adjustments, and those border tax adjustments will affect our trade with the Asia-Pacific, they will affect our partners. Our partners will want to know what is going on, they will want some input, even though this is a domestic American issue. We can have pro-competitive, wonderfully beneficial U.S. corporate tax reform. I actually think that this committee and people interested in the Asia-Pacific should be part of that discussion. Thank you.

[The prepared statement of Mr. Scissors follows:]

Statement before the House Committee on Foreign Affairs
Subcommittee on Asia and the Pacific
Hearing: "Step or Stumble: The Obama Administration's Pivot to Asia"

Trumping Obama in US-Asia Economic Relations

Derek Scissors
Resident Scholar

December 6, 2016

East Asia's population exceeds two billion, and including South Asia pushes the number to over half the global total. The world's second- and third-largest national economies are in East Asia, and India, in South Asia, will inevitably compete with them. In Southeast Asia, the combined population of Indonesia, the Philippines, and Vietnam exceeds 450 million, and all three have the potential to sustain better than 5% GDP growth. President Obama clearly and correctly made US relations with the Asia-Pacific a high priority.

The Obama administration, however, made errors of omission and commission. These errors could be corrected by Donald Trump's incoming administration in tandem with the new Congress,. If they are corrected, it would help improve both the American economy and America's economic role in the Asia-Pacific. The central actions the Trump administration and Congress should take are:[1]

(1) Let the TPP go. It was a very good but possibly infeasible idea, with a weak outcome. Make new trade rules only if they definitely help Americans.

(2) Do not try to zero out the trade deficit. It will not create jobs.

(3) Propose substantial steps forward on trade and investment in the Asia-Pacific. These can range from difficult, bilateral free trade negotiations to Japan to narrower talks on the food sector with Indonesia.

(4) Consider quick action, such as commercial bans, in response to China's intellectual property (IP) theft. Document Chinese subsidies, including but not focused on currency, to inform ensuing policy choices.

(5) Adopt unilateral measures that will bolster the American economic role in the Asia-Pacific, from lowering self-defeating US trade barriers to corporate tax reform.

The Past Eight Years

The Obama administration's main economic initiative in the Asia-Pacific was, of course, the Trans-Pacific Partnership (TPP). The TPP was absolutely the right idea—the US would certainly benefit from deeper and more secure market access in East Asia. And a successful initial round featuring Japan, Malaysia, and Singapore would have been a powerful lure for Indonesia, among others. Those supporting the TPP, starting with but certainly not limited to the Obama administration, had some sound reasons to do so.[2]

The final text of the TPP unfortunately fell well short of high aspirations. This may have been unavoidable with such a diverse group of countries. Whatever the reason, qualitative and quantitative assessments of the TPP estimated insignificant economic gains for the US.[3] In particular, the extent of national exemptions from the liberalization of services trade means that, despite being the world's most competitive services exporter, the US could expect only very small increases in services exports. The TPP would need to be considerably improved to be worthwhile for the US economically.

Partly as a result of this serious shortcoming, the Obama administration and its allies took to praising less tangible aspects of the TPP. Most of these are diplomatic in nature. My testimony does not address diplomacy, but it should be self-evident that the first "21st-century trade agreement," involving a dozen countries and three of the four largest US trade partners, cannot be a diplomatic initiative first and a trade initiative second or third. This implicit dismissal of its importance is a poor way to make the case for open trade and likely to foster rather than combat protectionist sentiment, especially when economic gains do not become visible.

A concrete illustration is the refrain concerning the need to make the rules.[4] This seems to suggest eventual commercial benefit but, in that case, just making rules cannot be the end in itself. Rules must offer at least a possibility of greater income for American companies and workers. The TPP fell short on this score, most notably in weak restrictions on state-owned enterprises, which could easily be circumvented by a country committed to protecting its firms from competition.[5]

Table 1. SOEs in World's Top 50 Companies, 2015

Ranking	Company Name
2	Sinopec (China)
4	CNPC (China)
7	State Grid (China)
18	ICBC (China)
26	Gazprom (Russia)
28	Petrobras (Brazil)
29	China Construction Bank (China)
36	Agricultural Bank of China (China)
37	China State Construction Engineering (China)
38	Japan Post Holdings (Japan)
39	PDVSA (Venezuela)
43	Lukoil (Russia)
45	Bank of China (China)
47	Pemex (Mexico)
50	Fannie Mae (United States)

Source: Fortune, "Global 500, 2015," http://fortune.com/global500/.

The Obama administration's emphasis on rules also does not hold up well in light of its failure to enforce existing US law. As perhaps the most painful example, IP theft has cost legitimate American companies something on the order of $2 trillion in total sales over the past eight years.[6] The administration joined Congress in creating the Defense of Trade Secrets Act but has done almost nothing to sanction IP thieves. No sanctions been applied in response to cyber espionage under the new authority provided in the 2015 National Defense Authorization Act;[7] even the mandated report has not been submitted. This passivity has been a mistake and change will benefit the US.

What *Not* to Change: Imports Are Not Losses

The rhetoric of the Trump presidential campaign can be taken as suggesting a goal to limit trade. This would be self-defeating. Americans voluntarily choose to participate in trade and do so because they prosper from it. This includes buying imports as much as making exports. The most fundamental issue, which drives decisions about trade agreements and sanctions, is how to treat the trade deficit.

The Trump campaign website approvingly quoted the Economic Policy Institute, which makes conventional protectionist arguments in sync with those made by organized labor.[8] The arguments depend almost entirely on the idea that a trade deficit automatically means lost jobs. This is wrong.

After the US fell into the Great Depression, the Congress passed sweeping tariffs in 1930. And the US ran large trade surpluses from 1929 to 1935 and 1937 to 1941.[9] Neither the tariffs nor the large trade surpluses helped the economy. While that was 75 years ago, in 2009 the economy crashed, and the trade deficit crashed with it. Trade became more balanced, as protectionists want, yet

Figure 1. US Trade Deficit vs. Unemployment Rate, 1975–2015

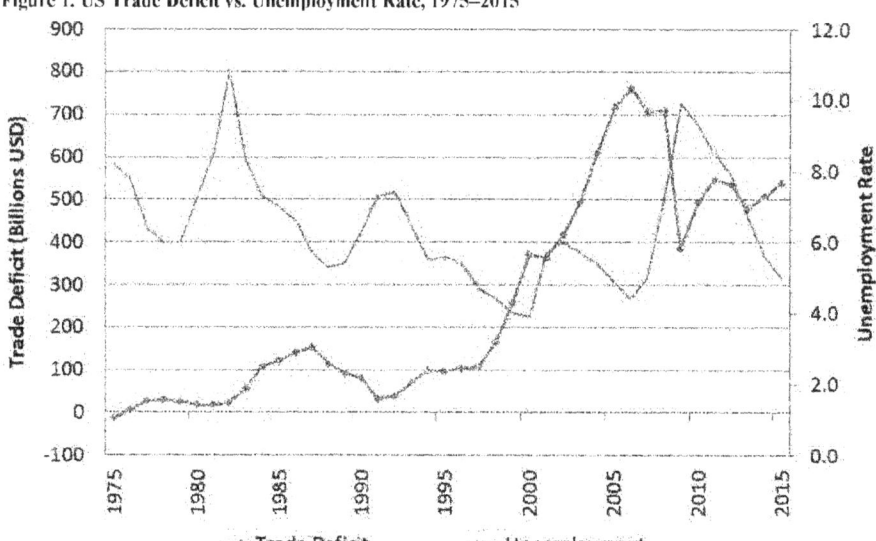

Sources: US Census Bureau, "U.S. Trade in Goods and Services," February 5, 2015, http://www.census.gov/foreign-trade/statistics/historical/gands.pdf; and US Bureau of Labor Statistics, "Labor Force Statistics from the Current Population Survey," March 28, 2016,

unemployment soared. The explanation is simple: when Americans are poorer, they buy fewer imports. Lower imports are not a sign of success.

The pattern extends far beyond 1930 and 2009. There is no statistical relationship between the trade deficit and unemployment from 1975 to 2015, no evidence that the trade deficit means lost jobs over the most recent 40 years (see Figure 1). This applies to the raw trade deficit figure and the deficit as a percentage of gross domestic product (GDP). It applies to trade and employment measures during the same year and to trade one year and employment the next.[10]

Because protectionists cannot link the trade deficit to jobs, they link it to GDP.[11] There is nothing magical about GDP; it is just an accounting tool. One view of GDP considers (in isolation) all imports to be harmful—every dollar of imports reduces GDP by a dollar. Because GDP is just accounting, this can be technically true. It's also ridiculous: if the US Navy blockaded our own ports, GDP would rise?

The next step in this flawed view is to assume GDP brings jobs. But GDP cannot cause job changes; as an accounting device, it cannot cause anything. Judging by GDP growth, 2010 should have been an excellent time for jobs.[12] Unemployment only fell that year because people gave up looking for work. You cannot save or spend your share of GDP because it has no value in the real world. GDP per person rose in 2010, but most people earned less money.[13] Using GDP to say trade should be balanced is a trick used by special interests because they cannot make the direct link to jobs. The Trump administration should set it aside.

What to Change: China

If the trade deficit is set aside as an issue in itself, sound policy can emerge. Regardless of the trade deficit, for example, the first five years after NAFTA went into effect saw *lower* unemployment, higher labor force participation, higher manufacturing employment, and higher manufacturing wages.[14] In

Figure 2. Manufacturing Employment, 1990–2015

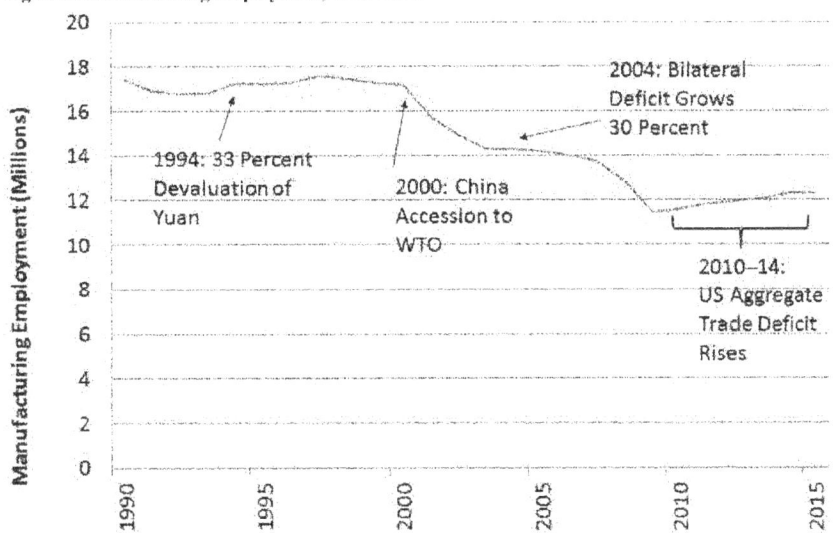

Source: US Bureau of Labor Statistics. "Labor Force Statistics from the Current Population Survey." March 28, 2016, http://data.bls.gov/timeseries/LNS14000000.

contrast, American manufacturing jobs were lost when China entered the World Trade Organization—2.9 million from just 2001 to 2003 (see Figure 2). While these were not all due to China, some were.[15] Policies regarding China can save American jobs, but only if we choose the right ones.

As an illustration, the Chinese yuan's exchange rate against the dollar did not drop at all while manufacturing jobs were being crushed. Later, from the middle of 2005 through 2008, the yuan rose as American currency critics want it to. (It was flat in 2009.) Yet the US job situation deteriorated starting in 2007. Labeling China a currency manipulator is technically accurate. At the time of writing, Beijing is allowing the yuan to fall. If sustained, this would call for US sanctions.[16] But focusing on the yuan would be a mistake. As with trade deficits, no long-term relationship can be found between China's currency and American jobs. Jobs were lost in 2001 with a stable exchange rate, and a weaker dollar was no help in 2007.

Examining trade in isolation, the biggest problem is Chinese subsidies, which is point 6 of the Trump campaign trade plan. When imports are cheap, Americans at least gain from low prices. When Beijing effectively blocks American exports, it is a pure loss for the US. China subsidizes its own firms and harms others in two main ways: (1) with basically no-cost loans from state-owned banks and (2) by preventing competition with state-owned enterprises (SOEs) in industries from insurance to machinery.[17]

While the political emphasis is on trade, investment is increasingly important. Chinese investment in the US in 2016 will shatter the previous record and could amount to tens of billions of dollars annually for years to come.[18] Most of it comes from quasi-private corporations, so restricting SOEs would do little. Cutting across trade and investment is IP, which includes cyber espionage and protection of trade secrets (Trump trade plank point 7). Americans are the best innovators in the world and China the biggest innovation thief.[18] As noted, IP-related loss is probably the single most costly aspect of our commercial relationship with China.

In the case of IP, the simple solution is best: companies that benefit from stolen IP are breaking the law and should be banned, with the length of the ban depending on the amount of theft. In response to trade and investment barriers, the principle of reciprocity could be invoked. With Beijing blocking

Figure 3. Foreign Direct Investment in the US, Yearly Totals

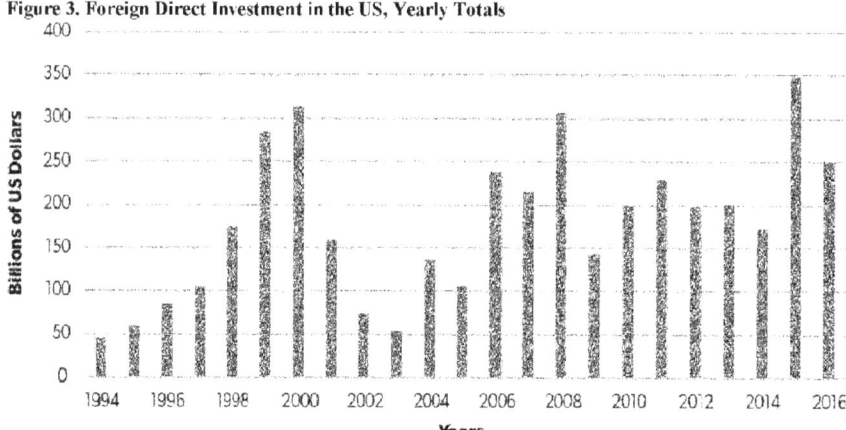

Source: US Department of Commerce, Bureau of Economic Analysis, "Foreign Direct Investment in the U.S.: Balance of Payments and Direct Investment Position Data," accessed November 14, 2016, http://www.bea.gov/international/di1fdibal.htm.

foreign participation in various sectors, the US has no obligation to permit unrestricted Chinese participation. When to insist on reciprocity, however, should be carefully considered. For one thing, the sectors that matter to the US are not the same as those that matter to China.

What to Change: Everyone Else

Trade issues sometimes get boiled down to China, which does a disservice to both trade and the American people. Despite mistakes in our policies, most Americans benefit from foreign trade and investment. Consumer goods are cheaper, permitting even the poor to own cell phones, for example. More Americans can be employed in industries such as agriculture and aviation because they export heavily.[20] Foreign investment in the US supports millions of jobs (see Figure 3). A China focus naturally leads to encourages limits on trade. A focus on the rest of the Asia-Pacific can lead to a (two-way) trade expansion that boosts our economy.

In this vein, the new administration's first action should not be applying tariffs. It should be assessing existing economic relationships in balanced fashion, opportunities as well as failures. In terms of opportunities, market size makes the Asia-Pacific the prime place to start. In terms of failures, detailed examinations of problems such as the extent of subsidies and IP theft are needed to make any sanctions effective. Smart negotiating requires good information, and gathering this information first will make all ensuing decisions more productive and credible.

It would greatly assure millions of Americans and dozens of our foreign partners, as well as wrong-foot critics, for the new administration to seek trade opportunities before or simultaneous with preparing any barriers. The president-elect has said he prefers bilateral agreements to multilateral agreements like the TPP.[21] Campaign rhetoric makes it difficult to imagine quickly moving toward new free trade agreements (FTAs) with developing economies, which feature cheap labor. But there are multiple developed economies in the Asia-Pacific worth contemplating: Japan, New Zealand, and Taiwan.[22]

New Zealand is the symbolic FTA. It's hard to imagine serious objections. Benefits would be similarly small, but it could be concluded quickly and would indicate to friends and allies a continued American commitment to free trade.

Bilateral talks with Japan would be entirely different. On top of opposition within the US, Japan has typically preferred multilateral arrangements and may well reject a bilateral FTA outright. On the other hand, a truly high-standard deal with Japan would offer hefty benefits, and the TPP embodies considerable progress toward such a breakthrough. Trump should inquire if Tokyo is interested.

Taiwan might be the happy Asia-Pacific compromise. It would be a worthwhile FTA—Taiwan is in the top 10 of American trade partners and global top 25 for GDP.[23] Yet Taiwan's tiny population means there is no job threat to the US (if transshipment is tightly restricted). Diplomatic risks in negotiating directly with Taiwan are paired with advantages in pressuring China. The island is a raucous democracy that may balk at open trade.[24] But our side looks good: congressional support for Taiwan is high, and boosted by President Trump having **Trade Promotion Authority**,[25] a Taiwan deal could sail through.

Beyond FTAs

Table 2. Countries Listed by Population

Rank	Country Name	Total Population
1	**China**	1,373,541,278
2	**India**	1,266,883,598
3	European Union	513,949,445
4	United States	323,995,528
5	**Indonesia**	258,316,051
6	Brazil	205,823,665
7	**Pakistan**	201,995,540
8	Nigeria	186,053,386
9	**Bangladesh**	156,186,882
10	Russia	142,355,415
11	**Japan**	126,702,133
12	Mexico	123,166,749
13	**Philippines**	102,624,209
14	Ethiopia	102,374,044
15	**Vietnam**	95,261,021

Source: CIA World Factbook, "Country Comparison: Population," accessed November 28, 2016, https://www.cia.gov/library/publications/the-world-factbook/rankorder/2119rank.html.

While FTAs are a clear way to assure the Asia-Pacific that the US is not withdrawing, they are certainly not the only option. It is vital that the US move forward in the region in some fashion. The areas of the world with the potential to grow most substantially are both in Asia: India and the Indonesia-Philippines-Vietnam nexus. Negotiations with any of them will be challenging, but even limited, issue-specific achievements could bring sizable long-term payoffs.

There are also unilateral actions to spur the American economy and our ties to the Asia-Pacific. The Trump administration could identify and lower harmful US barriers, such as the Jones Act, which raises the cost of all goods shipped to companies and consumers just to protect a few American companies.[26] Finally, the new administration and Congress will likely craft policies to boost international competitiveness, such as simplifying corporate taxes. Domestic policies are beyond the scope of this testimony, but they are in fact more important for the US.

Conclusion

The trade lesson from the Obama years is that a laudable vision cannot overcome the mistake of treating the economic benefits from trade as secondary. The TPP fell short economically and, despite being touted as strategic, therefore fell short politically. Similarly, apparently to avoid rocking the global boat, punitive action against China on IP and market access has been minimal, fostering resentment of trade among ordinary Americans. The US needs to return to seeking partners for genuinely open trade and investment, while tending to our own house.

Notes

[1] This testimony draws on my recent paper *The Art of the Trade Deal*. See Derek Scissors, *The Art of the Trade Deal*, American Enterprise Institute, November 17, 2016, https://www.aei.org/publication/the-art-of-the-trade-deal/.

[2] Derek Scissors, *What a Good Trans-Pacific Partnership Looks Like*, Heritage Foundation, March 8, 2013, http://www.heritage.org/research/reports/2013/03/what-a-good-trans-pacific-partnership-looks-like.

[3] United States International Trade Commission, "Trans-Pacific Partnership Agreement: Likely Impact on the U.S. Economy and on Specific Industry Sectors," May 2016, https://www.usitc.gov/publications/332/pub4607.pdf.

[4] The White House, Office of the Press Secretary, "Statement by the President on Trans-Pacific Partnership," press release, October 5, 2015, https://www.whitehouse.gov/the-press-office/2015/10/05/statement-president-trans-pacific-partnership.

[5] Derek Scissors, *Grading the Trans-Pacific Partnership on Trade*, American Enterprise Institute, December 9, 2015, https://www.aei.org/publication/grading-the-trans-pacific-partnership-on-trade/.

[6] The Commission on the Theft of American Intellectual Property, *The IP Commission Report*, National Bureau of Asian Research, May 2013, http://www.ipcommission.org/report/ip_commission_report_052213.pdf.

[7] United States House Committee on Rules, Rules Committee Print 113-58, House Amendment to the Text of S. 1847, December 2, 2014, http://www.armed-services.senate.gov/imo/media/doc/CPRT-113-HPRT-RU00-S1847.pdf.

[8] Donald J. Trump for President Inc., "Trade," https://www.donaldjtrump.com/policies/trade/.

[9] National Bureau of Economic Research, http://www.nber.org/databases/macrohistory/rectdata/07/m07047.dat.

[10] These correlations ignore domestic productivity and income gains that could explain both trade and jobs. They are just the first step in trying to prove trade deficits represent lost jobs. The first step fails.

[11] Danny Vinik, "We've Been Worrying About the Wrong Deficit," New Republic, April 30, 2014, https://newrepublic.com/ article/117594/gdp-report-reminder-trade-deficit-hurting-growth.

[12] US Bureau of Economic Analysis, "Real Gross Domestic Product," https://fred.stlouisfed.org/series/A191RO1Q156NBEA.

[13] US Census Bureau, "Income, Poverty and Health Insurance Coverage in the United States: 2010," press release, September 13, 2011, https://www.census.gov/newsroom/releases/archives/income_wealth/cb11-157.html.

[14] US Department of Labor, Bureau of Labor Statistics, "Databases, Tables & Calculators by Subject," http://data.bls.gov/ timeseries/CES3000000003?data_tool=XGtable.

[15] David H. Autor, David Dorn, and Gordan H. Hanson, "The China Shock: Learning from Labor Market Adjustment to Large Changes in Trade" (working paper, National Bureau of Economic Research, January 2016), http://www.nber.org/ papers/w21906.

[16] Derek Scissors, *China Edges Toward a Big Mistake*, AEIdeas, November 22, 2016, https://www.aei.org/publication/china-edges-toward-a-big-mistake/.

[17] Derek Scissors, "The Importance of Chinese Subsidies," testimony before the Subcommittee on Economic Policy, Committee on Banking, Housing, and Urban Affairs, US Senate, December 11, 2013, http://www.banking.senate.gov/ public/_cache/files/87eaf06c-3510-4222-ae9b-f9bc243f3d2a/23C6AE00CC53D93492511CC744028B5E. scissorstestimony121113.pdf.

[18] Derek Scissors, *Chinese Investments in the United State*, American Enterprise Institute, June 2016, http://www.aei.org/ chinese-investments-in-the-united-states/.

[19] The Commission on the Theft of American Intellectual Property, *The IP Commission Report*.

[20] US Census Bureau, "U.S. International Trade Statistics," http://censtats.census.gov/naic3_6/naics3_6.shtml.

[21] William Mauldin, "Five Takeaways from Donald Trump's Trade Speech," *Wall Street Journal*, June 28, 2016, http://blogs.wsj.com/economics/2016/06/28/five-takeaways-from-donald-trumps-trade-speech/.

[22] Beyond the Asia-Pacific, I have previously advocated an FTA with the United Kingdom. Unfortunately, this would have to wait until the painfully slow exit from the EU is farther along.

[23] US Census Bureau, "Top Trading Partners—December 2015," https://www.census.gov/foreign-trade/statistics/ highlights/top/top1512yr.html.

32

[24] Michael Gold and James Pomfret, "Over 100,000 Protest in Taiwan over China Trade Deal," Reuters, March 30, 2014, http://www.reuters.com/article/us-taiwan-protests-idUSBREA2T07H20140330.

[25] Ian F. Fergusson and Richard S. Beth, *Trade Promotion Authority (TPA): Frequently Asked Questions*, Congressional Research Service, July 2, 2015, https://fas.org/sgp/crs/misc/R43491.pdf.

[26] Bryan Riley, "The Jones Act: Protecting Special Interests, Not America," Heritage Foundation, June 15, 2016, http://www.heritage.org/research/commentary/2016/6/the-jones-act-protecting-special-interests-not-america.

Mr. SALMON. Thank you.

Ms. Currie, you are also back for a second time, so welcome, and thank you.

STATEMENT OF MS. KELLEY CURRIE, SENIOR FELLOW, PROJECT 2049 INSTITUTE

Ms. CURRIE. Thank you, Mr. Chairman. And I also want to echo the plaudits of your colleagues and your leadership of this committee—subcommittee, and note that you will be missed and your leadership will be missed. Thank you to all the members of the committee. I do want to submit my written testimony for the record.

Mr. SALMON. Without objection.

Ms. CURRIE. With one small correction that I have already noted to your staff.

The views that I am presenting today are my own and not necessarily those of Project 2049 Institute or its other scholars, but I am, nonetheless, grateful for the opportunity to share the them with you today.

Since Donald Trump's election victory last month, there has been a great deal of commentary on the future of the Obama administration's pivot to Asia. While the focus on the degree to which the pivot will continue under Donald Trump is important, much of this discussion has tended to focus on hand-wringing about President-elect Trump, while ignoring the serious deficiencies of the Obama administration's policies, both in terms of the conceptual failures, and the failures of the implementation.

The whole furor around the call nicely highlighted one the most serious conceptual weaknesses of the pivot. The failure to link intensified engagement in the Asia-Pacific with fundamental principles that historically have undergirded successful U.S. foreign policy for decades. These principles include privileging relationships with those countries that share our fundamental values; basing policy decisions on the way the world is, not how we wish it would be; operating based on an understanding and appreciation of both the importance and the limits of U.S. leadership; and making sure U.S. commitments are backed up with serious sense of purpose, and the resources necessary to reassure partners.

The Obama administration was intermittent at best in its adherence to these principles in Asia. And this inconsistency was tantamount to abandonment for those who rely on American strength, and those who seek to undermine it.

Asia's un-democratic leaders seem to understand opportunities are created by the gap between rhetoric and reality, and showed a consistent willingness to step into and exploit that gap for their own gain.

Looking around the region, it is hard to argue that on balance, there has been an improvement in terms of human rights and democracy, the subject I have been asked to speak to on today's hearing.

In particular, in the past 6 years, since the Obama administration launched the rebalance, China's party state has embarked on the most extensive campaign of repression since the cultural revolution, and has firmly closed the door on any prospect of political liberalization under CCP rule. Even in the Obama administration's poster child for the pivot, Burma, the Tatmadaw appears to be engaging in ethnic cleansing in Rakhine state, while simultaneously intensifying attacks on communities in Kachin and Shan states. Meanwhile, the Obama administration, having given away all potential leverage by prematurely lifting sanctions on the military, watches helplessly as Aung San Suu Kyi struggles with an unreconstructed Tatmadaw that has retained control over the key levers of power in the country. And I want to note Mr. Chabot's excellent work on Burma, and hope that that will continue going forward.

As the Obama administration drops serious U.S. commitments to support human rights and democracy across Asia in favor of an amorphous people-to-people pillar in the rebalance, abusive authoritarian regimes sought not only to normalize their behavior toward their own citizens, but engaged in broader efforts to normalize such abusive behavior within the international system.

Both the U.S. and the U.N. system have utterly failed to address the challenge of authoritarian rights abusing regimes that are immune to criticism and international mechanisms. In the case of China, the U.N. essentially has given up on its human rights mechanisms, so it is little wonder China's neighbors view U.N. criticism with thinly disguised disdain.

By failing to consistently and vigorously stand up for human rights and liberal values in the Asia-Pacific, and within the international system, the U.S. has created an environment where authoritarians feel empowered to argue that their legal, political, and moral perspectives are equally valid, or perhaps even better choices for the countries of the region and beyond. The idea that we can best support democracy and human rights in Asia by not talking about them, or by casting our own values as just one option among any number of other valid choices has proven to be manifestly false.

Going forward, I would like to make some suggestions on how we can craft a more realistic, yet also fundamentally idealistic foreign policy toward the Asia-Pacific and broader Indo-Pacific region. Such an approach would benefit not only the U.S. interest over the long term, but would also support a firmer foundation for regional peace and security.

We should start any deliberation on our policy choices from the premise that our values are our interests. When faced with competing policy choices, the one that adheres most closely to our values should be weighted accordingly. I would also note that free trade works best with free nations. Economic freedom should be a two-way street, and that is impossible when one partner is an authoritarian government. And many of the points that Derek has raised relate directly to this premise.

Our alliances need to move beyond the hub and spokes system to become truly networked in a way that revolves less around the U.S., and is more based on the reality of regional peace and security needs.

Diplomacy has got to stop meaning we pretend some unpleasant situation will just go away on its own, or get better if we ignore it, or use misleading euphemisms to discuss it with our partners.

The U.S. Foreign Service and our governance and democracy assistance programs need root-and-branch reforms to deal with this new reality.

Finally, I would add that we need to have Congress reassert itself as a strong voice in support of human rights and democratic values and U.S. foreign policy. Several recent policy errors in Asia might have been avoided entirely if the administration had treated Congress in a less highhanded fashion, and genuinely consulted with its members and staff before making policy decisions. Thank you very much.

[The prepared statement of Ms. Currie follows:]

Prepared Statement by Kelley Currie
Senior Fellow, Project 2049 Institute

House Committee on Foreign Affairs
Subcommittee on Asia and the Pacific

December 6, 2016

"Step or Stumble: The Obama Administration's Pivot to Asia"

Thank you Chairman Salon and Ranking Member Sherman for the opportunity to appear before the committee today to discuss the critical issue of US policy toward Asia. The views I am presenting today are my own, and not necessarily those of the Project 2049 Institute or its other scholars, but I am nonetheless grateful for the opportunity to share them with you all today.

Since Donald Trump's election victory last month, there has been a great deal of commentary on the future fate of the Obama administration's "pivot to Asia." Over the weekend – with a single phone call – the President-elect already seems to be signaling his intention to make good on his threats to shake up the foreign policy world and its often-peculiar habits. The apoplectic pearl-clutching over Mr. Trump's phone call with Taiwanese President Tsai Ing-wen is likely to further reinforce the view within the Trump camp that the practice of US foreign policy in Asia, if not globally, has become deeply warped and such a shake up is long overdue. And it is true that the manner in which we have allowed diplomatic fictions -- such as those that control our engagement with the democratically elected government in Taiwan – to dictate key aspects of US foreign policy is both fundamentally absurd and ultimately counterproductive. I personally welcome some fresh thinking about how we order our affairs in the region, particularly if it does not involve reflexive genuflections to avoid tantrums by Beijing's unelected dictators.

While the focus on the degree to which President-elect Trump's Asia policy will differ from his predecessor's is important, much of this discussion has tended to focus on hand-wringing about President-elect Trump while ignoring the serious deficiencies of the Obama administration, both in terms of conceptual failures and the failures of implementation. The furor around "the call" nicely highlighted one of the most serious conceptual weaknesses of "the pivot": the failure to link intensified engagement in the Asia-Pacific with fundamental principles that historically have undergirded successful U.S. foreign policy for decades. These principles include: privileging relations with those countries that share our fundamental values; prioritizing stronger alliance relationships over efforts to court leaders who are aggressively challenging US interests and regional peace and security; basing policy decisions on the way the world is, not how we wish it would be; operating based on an understanding and appreciation of both the importance and the limits of US leadership; and making sure US commitments are backed up with seriousness of purpose and the resources necessary to reassure partners. The Obama administration was intermittent at best in its adherence to these principles in Asia, and this inconsistency was tantamount to abandonment for both those who rely on American strength and those seeking to undermine it.

In particular, Asia's undemocratic leaders seemed to understand the opportunities created by this gap between rhetoric and reality, and showed a consistent willingness to step into and exploit that gap for their own gain. Looking around the region, it is hard to argue that, on balance, there has been an improvement in terms of human rights and democracy. In the 6 years since the Obama administration launched the "rebalance", China's party state has embarked on the most extensive campaign of repression since the

Cultural Revolution and has firmly closed the door on any prospect of political liberalization under CCP rule. From the arrests of scores of human rights defenders to the cult of personality around Xi Jinping to the confiscation of passports of Uighurs and Tibetans, the human rights situation in China has deteriorated dramatically with little comment or consequence from the Obama administration. Likewise, Beijing's systematic gutting of Hong Kong's autonomy has gone largely unremarked by this administration. With Beijing's compliance if not support, the Kim regime in North Korea has continued its brutal, autarkic rule at home while creating instability across the region with its nuclear provocations. The Obama administration's response: "strategic patience", which is diplo-speak for doing nothing.

In Cambodia, Hun Sen continues to rule through coercion and corruption, and the democratic opposition is facing existential threats that go virtually ignored by the Obama administration. In formerly democratic Thailand, the political situation remains deeply polarized, the army continues to rule after yet another coup, and the death of King Bhumibol (and drama around his succession) has heightened the sense of instability. In the Philippines, thousands of extrajudicial executions as part of President Duterte's war on drugs have grabbed international headlines, while his administration's pressure on press freedom and other civil liberties has garnered less global attention. And now in the Obama administration's poster child for the pivot -- Burma – the Tatmadaw appears to be engaging in ethnic cleansing in Rakhine state, while simultaneously intensifying attacks on communities in Kachin and Shan States. Meanwhile, the Obama administration, having given away all potential leverage by prematurely lifting sanctions on the military, watches helplessly as Aung San Suu Kyi struggles with an unreconstructed Tatmadaw that has retained control of the key levers of power in the country.

As the Obama administration dropped serious US commitments to support human rights and democracy across Asia in favor of the amorphous "people to people" pillar of the rebalance, abusive authoritarian regimes sought to not only normalize their behavior toward their own citizens but also engaged in broader efforts to normalize such abusive behavior within the international system. China's cross-border kidnappings in Thailand and Burma, as well as its aggressive international censorship efforts and its attempt to reshape the law of the sea through force, are the most obvious examples, but hardly the only ones. The Burmese military has successfully defined "democracy" downward to include a system where elected officials have no authority over a powerful military apparatus that effectively controls not only political and security matters, but also a major chunk of the economy. North Korea's ongoing provocations--and the international community's anemic response--have made a joke of the Obama administration's claims of progress on global nuclear proliferation. The UN system has utterly failed to address the challenge of authoritarian, rights-abusing regimes that are immune to its criticisms and mechanisms. In the case of China, the UN essentially has given up on using its human rights mechanisms, so it is little wonder China's neighbors view UN criticisms with thinly-disguised disdain. In pursuing the North Korea human rights Commission of Inquiry, one case where the UN has actually gotten under the regime's skin, the UN had to be dragged kicking and screaming, and the Commission struggles with a lack of support from key members of the P5. In those rare cases where some element of the UN tries to do the right thing, such as the ongoing bravery of UN special rapporteur on Burma Yang Hee Lee, the US and its European allies have been shamefully silent and unhelpful.

By failing to consistently and vigorously stand up for human rights and liberal values in the Asia-Pacific and within the international system, the US has created an environment where authoritarians feel empowered to argue that their political, legal and moral perspectives are equally valid or perhaps even better choices for the countries of the region and beyond. As we all know, democratic self-governance is hard work and the challenges of democracy do not necessarily get easier over time. But when the United States fails to defend democratic norms and ideals, we do a disservice not only to our own values but also to those who are struggling to realize those norms and ideals in other countries and contexts. Despite our failure to always live up to our own ideals, brave people who are sacrificing everything for democracy and human rights in other countries still look to us for inspiration and support. The idea that we can best support democracy and human rights in Asia by not talking about them, or casting our own values as just one option among any number of valid choices, has proven to be manifestly false. If this wrongheaded idea can be permanently consigned to the dustbin of failed foreign policy ideas, then at least one good thing would have come from this disastrous experiment.

Yet we also know that engagement on these issues with the diverse countries of the Asia-Pacific requires a deft approach that starts from an understanding of the interests and politics of each individual country. Approaching these countries from an overly-pedantic angle that assumes they have no agency of their own and are just waiting for the US to act is just as likely to lead to failure as approaching them based on narrow self-interests. We need to recognize that democratically elected leaders who are trying to promote long-term political liberalization at home should be engaged in a way that is wholly different from the manner in which we deal with illiberal regimes. In dealing with non-democracies, we need to be constantly aware of the fact that the interests of the leaders are far less likely to align with the interests of the people they claim to represent. Therefore, we should not feel the need to be as solicitous of the interests espoused or feelings claimed by authoritarian regimes. This is a particular challenge for working-level policymakers who only talk to the governments in the countries they are working on.

Going forward, I would like to make some suggestions on how we can craft a more realistic, yet also fundamentally idealistic, foreign policy toward the Asia-Pacific and broader Indo-Pacific region. Such an approach would benefit not only US interests over the long-term, but would also support a firmer foundation for regional peace and security.

- Start any deliberation on our policy choices from the premise that our values are our interests. When faced with competing foreign policy options, the one that adheres most closely to our values should be weighted accordingly. Opponents of values-aligned policy options should have to make an argument of why we are better off disregarding those values than preserving them -- not the other way around. More broadly, preserving the liberal international order is something that benefits the US and the world, and it is worth standing up for rhetorically and otherwise when necessary. We have got to stop apologizing for our values and start actively defending them if we actually believe they are important and meaningful. At the same time, every country in the region (and beyond) recognizes the rank hypocrisy of the way in which the United States and other western countries treats China's human rights record with kid gloves. These people are not stupid, and we should stop treating them like they are. Restoring American credibility on human rights in Asia has to start with a forceful and consistent approach to the ongoing crackdown on human rights in China, and a strong defense of those in the crosshairs of the Chinese regime at home and abroad.
- Free trade works best with free nations. Economic freedom should be a two-way street and that is impossible when one partner is an authoritarian government. While truly win-win agreements with democratic partners may be harder to do on the front-end, such agreements are fundamentally more stable, defensible and beneficial for all involved. Conversely, trying to engage in free trade with un-free nations has been greatly damaging not only for the United States but for millions of citizens in those countries as well. Illiberal regimes are able to force situations onto their citizens that free peoples would never accept. This element of coercion has no place in a world of economic freedom.
- Our alliances need to move beyond hub-and-spokes to become truly networked in a way that revolves less around the US and is more based on the reality of regional peace and security needs. This may mean new systems for allies in the short term that allows them to take on greater burden sharing over the long-term. It may also mean new kinds of relationships with countries such as India and Indonesia, who are not necessarily interested in becoming allies but are interested in shaping certain kinds of cooperation. It also means making sure that we are working most closely

with those allies who share not only our own values but those of our most important regional friends, and that we deeply listen to them about their threat perceptions and security needs.

- Diplomacy has to stop meaning that we pretend some unpleasant situation will go away or get better on its own if we ignore it or use misleading euphemisms to discuss it. This is as true in regard to the scaffolding of fiction around US relations with Taiwan as it is with the disaster that "see-no-evil" thinking has fostered in Thailand. Calling things by their right names has got to start being a bigger part of our diplomats' jobs; polite fictions politely delivered just don't cut it in a globally interconnected world where reality is readily available to contradict diplomatic wish-casting. The US Foreign Service and our governance and democracy assistance programs need root-and-branch reforms to deal with the new reality, and have for some time. Nowhere is this more apparent than in the Asia-Pacific.
- This change should start with how US embassies and aid programs deal with civil society in the region. Civil society in Asia is vibrant, effective and under constant threat; we need to be far more creative and resourceful in how we support them. Our diplomats should start with actually listening to CSOs – including and especially those that are critical of US policy -- instead of just engaging with the government. It would also help to recognize the unique role that civil society often plays in Asia as the only form of organized, peaceful opposition even within some democracies. One way to do that is to hire different kinds of people to work in our embassies, and set up different incentive structures that encourage new approaches to diplomacy.
- If we want international institutions to work in support of our interests, we have to invest in them and not only with money. We also need a reinvigorated effort to ensure that these institutions are based on truly universal values and operate accordingly. The US should support a top-to-bottom review to make sure that all UN bureaus, offices and mandates are consistent with the core values of the Universal Declaration of Human Rights, and advocate ending anything that does not make the grade. We need to fight for Taiwan to have a seat at the table as the democratically elected government representing the Taiwanese people. We need to support efforts to ensure liberal regional organizations are fully accredited to all UN bodies, and fight against efforts by governments like China to flood the zone with GONGOs or threaten independent civil society. Likewise when things at the UN actually are working, we need to really throw our weight behind them. Whether a special rapporteur is calling out the Kim regime's human rights abuses or investigating North Korea's proliferation practices, we need to back them up and make sure they have the tools they need to succeed. When lunatics are making death threats against Yang Hee Lee for speaking the truth about the situation in Burma, we need to take action to support her and her mandate. When the UN takes on responsibilities as it did in Cambodia and Timor Leste, we need to make sure those mandates are upheld to the fullest extent and not encourage it to take easy outs for political convenience.
- At the same time, we need to look at our relationship with ASEAN and evaluate whether we are making the most and best use of this regional grouping. Its inherent weaknesses as an organization put some hard limits on cooperation and we need to make sure that we are not wasting diplomatic capital on frivolous activities or missing opportunities for bi-lateral or mini-lateral cooperation because we feel the need to be sensitive to an over-hyped idea of "ASEAN centrality." Simultaneously we need to be working with those partners we do have within the grouping who can help to strengthen its most important elements, including its ability to resolve regional political conflicts – currently the weakest leg of the ASEAN stool.
- Finally, Congress needs to reassert itself as a strong voice in support of human rights and democratic values in US foreign policy. Several recent policy errors in Asia might have been avoided if the administration had treated Congress in a less high-handed fashion, and genuinely consulted with its members and staff before making a policy decision. By the same token, if Congress is not asserting its prerogatives, fully carrying out its oversight responsibilities and legislative responsibilities effectively, the foreign policy bureaucracy will continue to grind away doing the same thing it always has and getting the same mediocre results.

These are just a few of the things that can be done in the coming years to ensure that the US relationships in the Asia-Pacific region are built on a firmer foundation than the false equivalences of the Obama rebalance. While reorienting our policy in this way may appear destabilizing in the short term, I believe we will find that ultimately both our direct interests and the overall interests of regional peace and security will be better served by a more principled and less artificial engagement with the region. Like a democracy whose chaotic surface masks its underlying stability, whatever superficial turmoil may result from the initial adjustments to a more honest discourse would be more than made up for by having an Asia policy firmly rooted in values and principles. Thank you for the opportunity to share these thoughts and I look forward to your questions.

\###

Mr. SALMON. Thank you very much.

Mr. Lynn.

STATEMENT OF MR. BARRY C. LYNN, DIRECTOR, OPEN MARKETS PROGRAM, NEW AMERICA

Mr. LYNN. Thank you, Chairman Salmon, and thank you to the other members of the committee. I would also like to submit written testimony.

Mr. SALMON. Without objection.

Mr. LYNN. The Obama administration's pivot to Asia was a grave mistake. I say this not because I believe we can ignore Chinese provocations in Asia; we cannot, either in the South China Sea or the East China Sea or anywhere else. The pivot was a mistake because it focused mainly on countering military power with military power, but ignored the complex set of threats posed by China's use of trade power. China is a mercantilist nation that wields many political and economic tools to concentrate control over industrial capacity. Chinese leaders do so to provide jobs for their people, and to concentrate more money, hence more power in their hands. They do so also to be able to exert influence over nations that depend on that capacity, including the United States.

Over the last 5 years the Obama administration did nothing to address growing U.S. dependence on China for goods that Americans need every day; things like drugs, chemicals and electronics. On the contrary, the administration proposed a trade deal, the TPP, that if approved, would only have shifted certainly vital industrial capacity further into Chinese control.

Extreme concentration in China of vital industrial capacity exposes the United States to coercion by China, and may actually increase the likelihood of conflict by tempting Chinese leaders to take risks they would not otherwise take. Extreme concentration of industrial capacity by creating numerous single sources of supply, also raises the danger of cascading industrial crashes, much like the ones that crippled world production after the great Japanese earthquake of 2011.

Liberal trade has served U.S. interests in many ways since the Second World War, but in recent years, the uncontrolled shifting of jobs from the United States overseas has harmed millions of Americans. During this period, our national trade deficit has piled up dangerous levels of debt, and has provided Chinese leaders with cash they can use to increase China's influence in the world and to reduce America's. But to understand the full extent of the danger posed the radical shift in trade policy in the mid 1990s, we must look also at the structure of supply chains. We should study what exactly is made in China, and how much of any vital good comes from China. Looking at supply chains is what allows us to map our vulnerabilities in a time of conflict, and a way to judge whether the pivot to Asia was well-designed.

Twenty years ago, the United States depended on China for nothing that we needed day to day. But the U.S. embrace of WTO postnational trade policy in the 1990s freed China, often in alliance with large U.S. corporations to use trade power to consolidate control over many assembly activities and industrial components. This includes the basic ingredients for some of the Nation's important drugs, including antibiotics and some of the most vital inputs in our industrial food system such as ascorbic acid.

Given that private corporations often run their supply chains on a just-in-time basis in which goods are produced only as fast as they are consumed, there are often no backup supplies anywhere. The United States has long been in the practice of providing trade sanctions to other nations to achieve political ends. This includes, in recent years, North Korea, Iran and Russia. These sanctions are often highly effective. In 1956, the United States used trade sanctions to force Britain and France to pull their military forces out of Egypt after they attempted to seize the Suez Canal.

The extreme concentration of industrial capacities in China give leaders in Beijing the ability to impose similar sanctions on the United States in the event of an actual conflict, or even in the run-up to a potential conflict. What would the United States do in the event of such a cutoff of vital supplies? Would we try to tough it out? Would we cede to Chinese demands? Would we escalate to the use of cyber or military power? How would the public react? In every case, we have no idea what the answer might be. It appears that no agency of the U.S. Government has studied, in any depth whatsoever, the issue of U.S. industrial dependence on China.

Liberal U.S. trade policy in the half century to the mid 1990s helped provide the foundation for a period of unprecedented peace, and prosperity, and stability in the world. It is now clear that the extreme changes to U.S. trade policy in the 1990s upset those balances, in large part, by paralyzing the United States' ability to counter the mercantilist policies of China, and thereby to prevent a dangerous concentration of capacity, control, and power. Rather than waste more time on the TPP, or to attempt to treat a trade problem with military power, as we are largely doing with the pivot, the U.S. Government must figure out how to lessen our extreme and growing dependence on industrial capacity located inside China in ways that would make our Nation, indeed, the world as a whole, more politically and economically secure. Thank you.

[The prepared statement of Mr. Lynn follows:]

Barry C. Lynn
Director, Open Markets Program, New America
House Committee on Foreign Affairs: Subcommittee on Asia and the Pacific
Step or Stumble: The Obama Administration's Pivot to Asia
December 5, 2016

The Obama Administration's Pivot to Asia was a grave mistake. I say this not because I believe we can ignore Chinese provocations in Asia. We cannot, either in the South China Sea or the East China Sea. The Pivot was a mistake because it focused only on countering military power with military power, but ignored the complex set of threats posed by China's use of trade power.

China is a mercantilist nation that wields many political and economic tools to concentrate control over industrial capacity. Chinese leaders do so to provide more jobs for their people and to concentrate more money, hence more power, in their hands. They do so also to be able to exert influence over nations that depend on that capacity – including the United States.

Over the last five years, the Obama Administration did nothing to address U.S. dependence on China for goods that Americans need every day – things like drugs, chemicals, and electronics. On the contrary, the Administration proposed a trade deal – the TPP – that if approved would only shift more vital industrial capacity into Chinese control.

Extreme concentration in China of vital industrial capacity exposes the United States to coercion by China, and may actually increase the likelihood of conflict by tempting Chinese leaders to take risks they would not otherwise take. Extreme concentration of industrial capacity – by creating numerous single sources of supply – also raises the danger of cascading industrial crashes, much like the ones that crippled world production after the great Japanese earthquake of 2011.

Liberal trade has served the U.S. interest in many ways since World War II. But in recent years the uncontrolled shifting of jobs from the United States overseas has harmed millions of Americans. During this period, our national trade deficit has both piled up dangerous levels of debt and has provided Chinese leaders with cash they can use to increase China's influence in the world, and to reduce America's.

But to understand the full extent of the danger posed by the radical shift in trade policy in the mid 1990s we must also look at the structure of supply chains. We should study what exactly is made in China, and how much of any vital good comes from China. Looking at supply chains is what allows us to see the full extent of our vulnerabilities in a time of conflict, and a way to judge whether the Pivot to Asia was well designed.

Twenty years ago the United States depended on China for nothing that we needed day to day. But the radical changes in U.S. trade policy in the 1990s freed China – often in alliance with large U.S. corporations – to use trade power to consolidate control over many assembly activities and industrial components. This includes the basic ingredients for some of the nation's most important drugs, including antibiotics, and some of the most vital inputs in our industrial food system, such as ascorbic acid.

Given that private corporations often run their supply chains on a just-in-time basis, in which goods are produced only as fast as they are consumed, there are often no backup supplies anywhere.

The United States has long been in the practice of applying trade sanctions to other nations to achieve political ends. This includes in recent years Iran, North Korea, and Russia. These sanctions are often highly effective. In 1956 the United States used trade sanctions to force Britain and France to pull their military forces out of Egypt after they attempted to seize the Suez Canal.

The extreme concentration of industrial capacities in China give leaders in Beijing the ability to impose similar sanctions on the United States, in the event of an actual conflict, or even in the run up to a potential conflict.

What would the United States do in the event of such a cut off of vital supplies? Would we try to tough it out? Would we cede to Chinese demands? Would we escalate through the use of cyber or military power? How would the public react? In every case, we have no idea what the answer might be, as it appears that no agency of the U.S. government has studied the issue of U.S. industrial dependence on China in any depth whatsoever.

Liberal U.S. trade policy in the half century to the mid-1990s helped provide the foundation for a period of unprecedented peace and stability in much of the world.

It is now clear that the extreme changes to U.S. trade policy in the 1990s upset those balances, in large part by paralyzing the United States' ability to counter the mercantilist policies of China, and thereby to prevent a dangerous concentration of capacity, control, and power.

Rather than waste more time on the TPP, or to attempt to treat a trade problem with military power – as we are doing with the Pivot to Asia – the U.S. government must figure out how to lessen its extreme and growing dependence on industrial capacity located inside China, in ways that would make our nation – and indeed the world as a whole – more politically and economically secure.

Mr. SALMON. Thank you. When I first came to Congress in 1995, Warren Christopher was the Secretary of State. And I was on this Foreign Affairs Committee, a brand new member, and having done a lot of things in China and Taiwan, I'd been a missionary for the Mormon Church in Taiwan, the same time Jon Huntsman was, back in 1977 to 1979. So I remember asking the question of Mr. Christopher, Secretary Christopher, what is our policy toward China? And he said, well, it is strategic ambiguity. I listened to that and I tried to understand it, and I tried to understand it. And I guess they came up with the idea, that we basically just say that if you do something, we are not sure what we are going to do, but we will let you know afterward. That never worked in any other relationship I've ever had. I don't know why we think it works with China. But it has been the policy of multiple administrations to practice strategic ambiguity.

Dr. Ellings, you said that we needed more clarity. Where can we be more clear on things? And has strategic ambiguity served us well?

Mr. ELLINGS. I remember a Herblock cartoon when Christopher—I am giving away, I guess, our mutual ages here—but in any case, right after his first trip to China there was a Herblock cartoon in which Christopher was sitting before the President reporting, and his head was in his lap. China had basically eaten his shorts. But in any case—yeah, you might not be surprised, that I think we have a lot of specific things to do. I would start, number one, I mean, our credibility is everything. We need to rebalance truly, which means to end sequestration and make the investments we need to make appropriate responses to the challenges. We have not done a strategic assessment that is realistic, and we need one.

Credibility, as I said, is everything. We have got to work so hard with our allies, and win their unambiguous alignment with us.

I think also, we have to do something once we do the strategic assessment we—they are very specific things, UUVs, UAVs, more subs. We have to invest in these things. Burden sharing, frankly, has been raised by the President-elect; it is not unreasonable. I think our allies understand their common interest with us. I think as we define new things ahead, those—the burden sharing can proceed. And number one of anything else, I would put in THAAD, and anything else we need with regard to North Korea, and simply tell China, We are going to do this until you figure out that it is in your interest to end your support of their nuclear program. Only China has that capacity, and we have got to get THAAD in there and whatever else. It is the first leverage we really have. And so I am a huge, huge supporter of that. I can go on. Anyway, on the military side, that is what I——

Mr. SALMON. I actually share your enthusiasm for that. And one of my concerns is with some of the political problems that President Park is facing in South Korea that might jeopardize our deployment plans. I hope not; I hope this is something that the new administration really pushes, because we have done nothing to properly motivate China, who is the 800-pound gorilla in those Six Party talks with North Korea. North Korea has an overdependence on them for energy and food, and they could make the difference, but they have been unwilling to so far. And I think that motivates them in the right direction.

Mr. ELLINGS. I totally agree with your concern about the situation domestically in South Korea is jeopardizing that deployment. So we need a plan B. We need the deployment. If it is not on the peninsula, then where is it going to be? It is our only source of leverage, and frankly, we have to defend our allies. We will not be credible. This is a real threat. It is not theoretical; it's not down the road; it is the kind of poster child of the failure of the pivot.

Mr. SALMON. Ms. Currie, you talked a little bit about human rights. I remember when I first came to Congress, one of the raging debates was every June, we had Jackson-Vanik, where we would debate most favored trading status for China. And every year, it was kind of the same thing. And I remember when we had to push for PNTR, permanent normal trade relations with China. I think I had a private debate with Mr. Rohrabacher, and I remember saying to him that if we passed PNTR that because of constructive engagement, we would see phenomenal improvements in human rights and the like. I had just attended, not long before that debate, a hand-over ceremony for Hong Kong, and I had predicted that that would be a smooth transition, it really would be one country, two systems. And Mr. Rohrabacher, I will say to you right now, with egg all over my face, I was wrong. Those changes didn't materialize, they did for a time, under President Jiang Zemin, I think that he carried on a lot of the visions of Deng Xiaoping, and I think that he moved in the right direction. But the two presidents subsequent to him moved back the other way and they increased their iron grip on the people and reversed, I think, some very positive human rights improvements.

And so I ask you, Ms. Currie, without putting Jackson-Vanik back in place, I am not sure whether that is possible, how can we do an adequate job focusing on the issues of Hong Kong and their self-determination and human rights abuse and all the other things we really care about; how can we do that effectively?

Ms. CURRIE. I was a young congressional staffer during those discussions, and staffed one of your colleagues, Congressman John Porter, who joined you on that trip for the hand-over and engaged in these frequent discussions with Mr. Rohrabacher, and with you at that time. And there was a lot of genuine soul searching, I think, on both sides. I think that there was good faith belief on both sides, both against PNTR and in favor of it. There were many people who genuinely thought that their view on that was the way to improve the situation in Hong Kong.

I have recently had a number of conversations with a friend of mine, Jim Mann, who wrote a wonderful book about 10 years ago called The China Fantasy, that kind of talked about how we all wanted to believe that economic liberalization would bring political liberalization in China. I think that it comports with our values and with our ideas about how our own country is set up, and we just kind of instinctively appeal to people.

Unfortunately, we then didn't follow up by doing any of the things that could have actually made that a reality. And by—and that the opposite has happened, that the economic liberalization has strengthened the regime by giving it more tools for oppression, made it more powerful and more influential in the world. And now we have to deal with that reality. But the tools actually remain essentially the same going forward.

First of all, I think one of the—like I was saying before about the pivot, one of the fundamental mistakes was—and my colleagues sort of alluded to this here, that we tried to compete in the region in areas that are strengths for Beijing and relative weaknesses for us, for instance, on the economic playing field, and trying to displace China as an economic partner in the region somewhat. Whereas, you know, these things may or may not—we can argue about the relative strength of the U.S. and China and economics and military in the region. But one place where we clearly have an advantage over Beijing is on our values and our ideas. And yet, we abandoned that playing field for the past 8 years; we just left it there and didn't do anything.

What is remarkable when you travel around the region and get outside of China, within China, I just have to kind of set it on the side for now, but our ideals, even when we fall short of them ourselves—I am talking about human rights and democracy—are far more attractive to the people of the region than Beijing's authoritarian ideals, which are only attractive to other authoritarians. And when we stop talking about those ideas, and we stop defending the international order, people notice. It has an effect on them and their willingness to defend those ideas also. And this goes to trade, it goes to human rights, it goes to a whole host of issues that then make the whole problems harder for us, and open more doors for Beijing to have more influence in more countries in the region.

So I think that, kind of, as first principles, we have got to get back to proudly saying, yes, the United States believes in these ideas. And even when we don't always live up to our ideals, they are still our ideals, and we are willing to defend them and fight for them, not just rhetorically, but by other means as necessary, and that is where the resources that Dr. Ellings talked about come in, and being able to back up or commitments to our allies, privileging relationships with allies that share our values, privileging not just military alliance relationships, but also trade relationships with those who share our values, which then are also easier because we have shared platforms for understanding how to get along with each other, and trade with each other, and then backing those up with real meaningful things, and having consequences on the other side for those who don't share our values.

Mr. SALMON. Thank you very much. I recognize Mr. Bera.

Mr. BERA. Thank you, Mr. Chairman.

As I look back on the last 8 years, there are some areas that I think have been pretty successful. Obviously, I am a firm believer in the pivot to Asia. I do think we can look at kind of the renewed vigor in the U.S.-India relationship as an area of opportunity, not necessarily a straight shot, but clearly where we are today compared to where we were 8 years ago, but the opportunities. Some of this is on the Indian side with the ascendancy of Prime Minister Modi, and some of the reforms he is trying to make domestically. That is clearly an area that I do think we have had some success. That said, it is a region fraught with challenge. And I know many of us sit with an open mind with the incoming administration, you know, and are very open to how they will approach the region, but they are going to have to hit the ground running. I mean, we have talked a lot about China. We have touched on the complexity in North Korea. The internal challenges that are facing Korea as they address some of their political turbulence.

We look at a new administration in the Philippines. We still got major unresolved issues in the South China Sea and how to approach that from a position of strength. And that is an area that I have disagreed with the administration on, I think. It is much more difficult for us to resolve the South China Sea today than had we approached it much more aggressively 1 year, or 2 years ago. With that said, we are where we are. And going forward, I think there are a couple of things that we have to do and the panel has touched on the importance of reassuring our allies about our commitment to the region.

Our economic commitment, our diplomatic commitment, the commitment of our military assets as well. I think it is very important not to be ambiguous about our commitments to our allies, but to be very clear that we are there with them.

We have to understand that it is going to be a shared commitment, with countries with similar sets of democratic values, you know, countries like Australia, New Zealand, et cetera, that it won't be the United States in this commitment by themselves. It will be a shared commitment.

We also have to be—you know, the TPP is where it is at. As someone who supported the President's ability to go out and negotiate the deal. We are where we are.

And there is a lot of rhetoric on the campaign trail on both sides. I think we have to explain the benefits of opening up global markets to our own domestic, you know, community first, to our workers and make sure if we are negotiating these deals and moving forward, that we are explaining the benefits in job creation, that people are understanding that. And that everyone, you know, from the frontline workers to the shareholders are benefiting equally from, you know, opening up these markets. But the reality is, we can't withdraw and have an isolationist policy. These are the fastest growing markets in the world.

On a fair playing field, I will put U.S. companies and U.S. workers up against anyone. The criticism of prior deals and perhaps even TPP is because we weren't always on a fair playing field. And that was fine maybe in the 20th century when we could be a bit more benevolent, we could, you know, allow countries like Japan and others to rebuild. But we are in a competitive global environment now. We have to make sure that the deals we are negotiating are fair and balanced, not just for the countries we are trading with, but for our own workers.

I have taken up a lot of my time without asking a question.

You know, maybe, Dr. Scissors, you talked about the danger of having an isolationist trade policy. And maybe if you could just touch on some that for our own domestic population, why that would be a bad—this would be a bad time to withdraw from the world.

Mr. SCISSORS. Well, I will try to do so quickly. I think—and also because you touched on part of this, these are the fastest growing economies in the world. The Philippines is probably number one now. India, because of recent internal steps is probably going to be number two. Vietnam is there as well. Indonesia is a little lower, but it is also 250 million people. That is a nice market.

If we want opportunities for our workers beyond the American market, the American market is the most important in the world, but if we want to add to that, the Asia-Pacific is where it is at. And I think, you know, everybody on this committee understands that.

So I think what you want to say is use some of the language that people have used so far, which is to say 1 billion more consumers. You have 350 million consumers in the U.S. You have three times that many more that you could add, to give people some idea of what is out there. But, and this is where we haven't succeeded, couple that with the concrete steps we are actually taking to take advantage of it.

I am picking on the Obama administration a little bit here, because I am trying to make a larger point, which is when you talk about markets and you talk about dynamism, you then don't go back to talking about diplomacy and strategic gains. That doesn't deliver gains to American workers. You have to say what is in the agreement is not a rule that we make instead of China. What is in the agreement is rules that open our markets and get us the following benefits.

And I think what is missing and what might be easier, as we discussed here and as has been discussed in the campaign, it might be easier to do this bilaterally. It was a really difficult undertaking the Obama administration went to bringing such disparate countries together, Japan, Vietnam, Canada, Peru. I mean, this is really hard. And so maybe the way to do this both in terms of success, the solidity of the agreement and the communication is to say, look, let's simplify it. This is one country that is growing rapidly and has a lot of people; there are a lot of opportunities for us, this is concretely how we are going to do it.

I do not, as I said, fault the Obama administration at all for trying TPP. From the country's standpoint, we need to learn why it didn't work. Why both major presidential candidates opposed it. And my response is, we couldn't deliver concrete economic benefits. We do this bilaterally, we can't necessarily have the giant benefits you are talking about, but step-by-step, start with one bilateral agreement, add another. Who wants to negotiate with us first.

As Kelley said, who are our best partners in terms of values? I think we can go back and say, look, each of these agreements are with good partners that have created opportunities. Each step may be small, but we are heading toward the Asia-Pacific being open, and all that potential benefit that everyone here sees.

Mr. SALMON. Thank you.

Mr. Brooks.

Mr. BROOKS. Thank you, Mr. Chairman. I am going to miss you.

Mr. SALMON. I will miss you too.

Mr. BROOKS. I hope things go well in Arizona.

Recently, President-elect Donald Trump had a telephone conversation with President Tsai Ing-wen of Taiwan. And many in the news media and diplomatic community went apoplectic. I would like for you to, please, share your view on whether Donald Trump's phone call with the Taiwan President was wise or unwise, advanced or retreated the interests of America? And I will just work my way across.

Dr. Ellings?

Mr. ELLINGS. Sure. I am very, very pleased to answer that question. As you say, it has been, I think, basically a tempest in a teapot. But, yeah, there has been a lot of hot air and so on expended on this.

First of all, there are strategic as well as democratic value reasons you might want to refurbish a relationship with Taiwan. China has put tremendous pressure on Taiwan. It is not in an enviable strategic position. At the same time, it has developed a remarkable democracy.

I happened to be by the way, Chairman Salmon, also at Tsai Ing-wen's inauguration. There are strategic realities that strike fear in many Americans' hearts, but my view is, I think, a sober one that this actually—this call to a still President-elect Trump is strategically useful, justified. There is no reason we can't have conversations while in the meantime China can act so aggressively and feel impervious to these kinds of things.

Mr. BROOKS. All right. Thank you, Dr. Ellings.

And I am going to work around a little bit. Each of you have about a minute. But the folks on my right haven't had much time. So I am going to go to Mr. Lynn then Ms. Currie and to Dr. Scissors.

Mr. Lynn?

Mr. LYNN. I basically agree that the President-elect Trump's taking of that phone call was probably a good thing. And, you know, one of the things that all of these nations, in that region, have not been talking about but need to talk about is the fact that all of their industrial systems are so entirely interdependent. I mean, for the same reason that it is dangerous for the United States to—for the Obama administration to pretend that there might be a military solution in the South China Sea or the East China Sea is just as dangerous for the Chinese to believe that there is a military solution, vis-a-vis Taiwan.

Any military action in that zone by the United States, by the Japanese, by the Chinese, will create an immediate disruption of supply systems on which we all depend, and will, within a matter of days, seize up the entire world's industrial system.

Mr. BROOKS. Mr. Lynn, thank you for your insight. I am trying to reserve some time for Ms. Currie and Dr. Scissors.

Ms. Currie.

Mr. CURRIE. Thank you. I think it was both the right thing to do and a smart thing to do for the reasons that my colleagues have indicated. And also because—you know, one of the things that drives me the most crazy, as a former State Department employee, is the tendency we have to use euphemisms and construct these, you know, world scaffolds around what we do that don't have any connection to reality.

And with a single phone call, President-elect Trump and Tsai Ing-wen together—she had agency in this, which is another thing that people seemed to completely miss, that she was the other party on the other end of the phone call who made a decision to do this as well. But, you know, this is—they kind of blew that up a little bit. And that was very well done and warranted, I think.

Mr. BROOKS. Thank you.

Dr. Scissors?

Mr. SCISSORS. I will be brief. I don't really care about the phone call. What I want to see is what U.S.-Taiwan relations are going to look like in a Trump administration. If the phone call says the Trump administration is going to be more active in talking to Taiwan about issues in the South China Sea, about arms sales, about what I would like to talk about, which is improving the economic relationship, that is fantastic, then it is a great idea.

If it is just something that occurred while he is still a private citizen, and we don't act with the Taiwanese, then it doesn't mean anything and it doesn't add up to anything. I would even say, I am perfectly happy talking to the mainland while we are talking to Taiwan. They want to be involved in the conversation, fine. As long as the U.S. is talking to Taiwan figuring out where we can cooperate more, that is what matters. If this was the first step, great.

Mr. BROOKS. All right. Thank you for your insight.

Mr. SALMON. Thank you.

Ms. Gabbard.

Ms. GABBARD. Thank you, Mr. Chairman.

Thank you all for being here.

I am going to keep my question brief, because I would like to hear responses. But my question is about North Korea. I represent Hawaii. We are in the middle of the Pacific and within range of North Korea's intercontinental ballistic missiles. And obviously, the continued progress that they make in miniaturizing their nuclear weapons is deeply, deeply concerning.

Everyone talks about how essential China is to the denuclearization of North Korea, but very few people have any concrete ideas on exactly how to get China to take action, to actually change the dynamic here. So if each of you could just comment briefly on that question and taking into account what is happening on the peninsula and the relationship between the peninsula and Japan and China and us.

Mr. ELLINGS. Shall I start?

Ms. GABBARD. Yes.

Mr. ELLINGS. Thank you so much. Well, you just kind of asked me to talk about my favorite subject. I have been writing and thinking about this literally for 30 years.

And so I think it boils down to this—by the way, I live in Seattle. And Seattle also, in those concentric rings, has JBLM, which are forces to reinforce the peninsula. The Bangor Trident Missile Base, we are just like you, a number one target. So I feel it personally.

My view, as I stated earlier, is that the clearest thing we can do, in which the Chinese have obviously signaled they would like us least to do, is get THADD into South Korea. And I would put in a broader antimissile system combining Japan at sea and on the peninsula. We expressed earlier concern that President Park's difficulties put at risk our ability, perhaps, next year to deploy THAAD there. That is a terrible development. I do worry about that. So we have to have plan B and C here.

But we have got to do it. And I will tell you not having learned from the INF issue and what we did in the early 1980s, that is something I think we all need to study here. If we had a robust antimissile system in northeast Asia, I think China would do what is necessary to denuclearize the north.

Mr. SCISSORS. I don't mean to avoid your question, but it is security, so I am going to yield to my colleagues.

Ms. CURRIE. I would add a couple of things. Go after the palace economy more vigorously—we have not implemented all the sanctions, the economic sanctions tools that we have in our disposal to go after North Korea's palace economy and hold the Chinese to account for their role in propping up the palace economy that surrounds Kim Jong-un and the people around him, and allows them to live in a lifestyle that is completely attenuated from the way that the rest of the North Korean people live.

So there are many things that we can do to make them more uncomfortable and put pressure on the regime in that way. And the Chinese don't like it, but, again, as Dr. Ellings said, we need to just tell them, look, this is what we are going to do. You aren't being helpful, and so we are taking these things into our own hands.

And then the other thing that I would do is throw everything we have diplomatically, politically that we can behind the U.N.'s commission of inquiry on human rights in North Korea, because that inquiry has gotten under the skin of the Kim regime in a major way. They really don't like being brought up in the U.N. on human rights charges, in this way, and it really bothers them. And I don't think we have fully explored the limits of how we can take advantage of that process.

The Chinese also don't like having to defend them at the U.N. and having to expend diplomatic capital on the North Koreans at the U.N. on human rights.

Ms. GABBARD. Thank you.

Mr. LYNN. Just adding to what Ms. Currie said, is supply lines matter. And one of the ways to exert pressure upon the North Koreans is to really push the Chinese to become serious about putting pressure on the North Koreans.

As we may remember in the run-up to the Iraq war, North Korea was acting in an extremely belligerent way, and there was a sentiment that they might have taken advantage of the focus of the U.S. military in the Middle East to engage in some kind of action in their area, and the Chinese cut off the supplies of a number of goods into North Korea, and that brought the North Koreans to heel.

Ms. GABBARD. Thank you.

Thank you, Mr. Chairman.

Mr. ELLINGS. I just wonder if I could just add something here——

Ms. GABBARD. Sure.

Mr. ELLINGS [continuing]. That I think is really important?

I think no pressure directly on North Korea will work. Direct pressure on North Korea, no matter how we have done it, their regime requires the nuclear weapon. And so there is no way direct pressure without pressure on China is going to work.

And China's interest—if we don't put enough pressure on China, China's interests are in North Korea as a buffer, and as North Korea as an irritant to us; it pins our troops down; it keeps our attention. If there is a war, it is another front. So North Korea is a core interest of China. And so what we have to make clear to China is we understand it is a core interest, but its nuclearization is our core interest.

Mr. SALMON. You know, it is interesting, they say that the reason they are hesitant to jump in and do what needs to be done is that it would destabilize North Korea, and there would be this onslaught of refugees coming across the North Korean border into China.

I think the real reason is that they fear a one Korea. They fear a unified Korea, and they fear an increased U.S. presence that is on the peninsula. So I think that is what the real issues are. And so I think that the provocative answers that have been given about motivating China are real, and they would work.

One of the things I have been pushing for the last year is the deployment of THAAD, and I think, as you said, Dr. Ellings, that increasing that to possibly Japan as well and other ballistic defense systems is absolutely imperative.

China is not going to care unless you make them care. And they are not going to do it out of the goodness of their hearts. They are only going to do it if they feel compelled to do it, because not doing it costs more than doing it. That is what the answer is.

Mr. Rohrabacher—oh, have I missed you? I am so sorry.

Mr. Perry. General Perry.

Mr. PERRY. Thank you, Mr. Chairman. Doing, as always, a fabulous job.

I am thinking about the conversation, initially, strategic ambiguity. And I am just wondering what appears to be—what is the President-elect's propensity for unpredictability. You know, strategic ambiguity in the sense that it was described by the chairman was essentially—we didn't know what the heck we were doing. But when you want to be ambiguous, knowing that you want to be that, is probably a strength, right?

So my question is, are there specific conditions that we should articulate like a floor or ceiling with China? And then remain ambiguous about some other things where maybe we remain—we maintain some flexibility to get them to head where we want to go? And I just want to—I would like to, actually, start with you, Mr. Lynn.

What are your thoughts on that? Are there some specific things that we should articulate, and what would they be?

Mr. LYNN. Well, one of the things that we absolutely want to articulate is that we—to increase the security of both the United States and China, to increase the security of all the nations in the region and indeed of the world, we want to reduce the number of cases in which all key components are located in China. And that is going to require the cooperation of the Chinese.

When you have all of the certain kind of chemical industry built up in China, the Chinese can do a lot to prevent us from moving any of that capacity abroad. We think of industrial activities as something that moves around. That is not the case. But it is in everybody's interest that industrial capacity be much more widespread. It creates a resilient system, and it means that when mistakes are made, as they will inevitably be made in human society, bad things are less bad.

Mr. PERRY. Ms. Currie.

Mr. CURRIE. Well, I will talk about something that we continually articulate as kind of a floor in the region with China, which is our statement that we will not accept China changing the status quo on Taiwan or militarizing the South China Sea by force or coercion. And we make these statements all the time, but then we don't actually do anything to back them up.

So I think we have floors. I think we have articulated them over time, but the Chinese don't actually see them as floors. It is not the problem that we don't have floors, it is just that they are very holey and not very stable and not very sturdy and not viewed by the Chinese as meaningful.

And so I think, again, being consistent, being public about what these basic things are is one thing, but then having meaningful consequences when the Chinese start to push on them and stomp on them and try to poke holes in them and making sure that we are doing things to push back.

And whether it is strengthening Taiwan's defenses, deploying THAAD, being more active in our regional diplomacy within ASEAN about the South China Sea issues, to push back on the salami-slicing tactics, negotiating more bilateral investment treaties, more bilateral trade agreements to encircle China with more open economic freedom, any and all of these things. You know, it is not an either/or we need to——

Mr. PERRY. Do you think that our inability as maybe you describe it—and so if I am describing it incorrectly let me know—but our ability to stand firm on how we articulate the barriers or the constraints that we have, is that a function of our governance, our form of governance, that we say one thing but we have a hard time—it requires legislation; it is not something the executive could do unilaterally? Is that what the deal is, or is that we talk big but then we don't follow through?

Mr. CURRIE. I think it is the latter. We have all the legislative tools in place. You have the Taiwan Relations Act, you have a Tibet Policy Act; you have a raft of legislative pieces over the history of the past 25 years.

Mr. PERRY. So it would be your opinion that the executive can make all the difference in this instance?

Ms. CURRIE. I think forceful leadership that is principled and consistent and actually has a plan for when things don't work out according to the fiction they have created in their head——

Mr. PERRY. Okay.

Dr. Scissors?

Mr. SCISSORS. Yes, I have two specific answers. And one is, I think we have already provided the ceiling. America's commitments to open markets have helped. It is not the main thing, but it has helped raised hundreds of millions of Chinese out of poverty. We have played our role in helping China's development for the past 35 years. So I don't think whatever we do going forward—anyone can doubt that the U.S. has tried to accommodate China and done well for the Chinese people in our policies to now. Where I would put the floor is to enforce American law. The Chinese steal intellectual property. They are breaking our law.

I will give you a small case but one that infuriated me. We had a Federal court a few months ago say the Chinese vitamin C makers can violate U.S. antitrust law, but they were told by the Chinese Government to do it, so they have sovereign immunity. That is outrageous. I am not a lawyer. I have no idea about the legal foundations of the decision. I am saying as a matter of policy, so the Chinese Government can tell Chinese companies to break U.S. law and it is okay?

I think our credibility on accommodating China to this point is extremely high. I can't imagine another country that would have run the global economy the way we did that would have helped the Chinese.

And the floor comes from, we have laws. You have to obey them, and I don't want to hear excuses about the government told you or not.

Mr. PERRY. Quickly, Dr. Ellings, with the chair's indulgence.

Mr. ELLINGS. Yeah, two quick comments. On the question of IP theft, the Congress and the President signed a bill that provided the power to respond with all the powers that the President has to stop terrorists in using the banking system and so on. The President has the power to stop IP thieves overseas and has not done it, so we have no credibility.

Number two. This is really a kind of the most important, I think, strategic point to make. Ambiguity is never what you want to have in a strategic situation, ever, unless you are forced into it out of weakness.

And so what my concern is, since we have not decided on a military strategy in Asia, we have not figured out what, in my view is, a plan to show unambiguously that with our allies we can win a battle in the commons without striking China directly, that is credible. If we have to strike China directly, then we are raising the specter of them striking back at our homeland. So we need unambiguous capacity to win over the commons, and that is the critical strategic issue facing us today.

Mr. PERRY. Thank you, Mr. Chair.

Mr. SALMON. Thank you.

Mr. Rohrabacher.

Mr. ROHRABACHER. This ambiguity stuff, I will tell you that— let's face it, when you talk about ambiguity, what they really mean is they don't know what the hell they are going to do. And it is not we don't know what our reaction are or we have a reaction that we don't want the enemy to know. We don't know.

I have been saying that for a number of years, and no one has ever come forward and say, well, let me tell you the secret plan. No one has ever done that.

It is fitting from the last hearing of this subcommittee that we note one thing, that we have been talking about the Pacific today and very little reference has been made to Japan. And Japan is the most important player in the region. And Japan, if there is going to be peace and prosperity, the United States has got to maintain its incredibly positive relation with Japan. And let us not end this hearing without reaffirming that because—and let me just note, and how could we actually send messages, then, in terms of China or North Korea? Well, I bet if we decided to aggressively and publicly support the rearming of Japan and the reintroducing of the Japanese Navy into the Pacific rather than putting that entire burden on the American taxpayers, I think there would be a message there, and it would be a message they would pay attention to.

So basically, perhaps as well, when the Chinese start stealing all of our technology, maybe then we could go to Japan and have a very open and—how do you say—mutually beneficial treaty that would then show that these other people are being left out because the Japanese are playing honestly with us now and are trying their very best to be good friends. So recognizing the role of Japan, I think, is essential when we try to plot out what is going on in the future.

Mr. Scissors, I certainly agree with you totally about the TPP. And let me just ask you whether or not you have looked at the patent section of the TPP? I was told over and, again, oh, no, there is nothing in there that would change the patent law of the United States.

Is it still in there, the provision that eventually I saw there, that said that we will endeavor to change our patent law, which right now means that when an inventor files for a patent, that patent is secret, until that—that patent application is secret until it is issued, until the patent is issued?

The TPP that I read said we will endeavor to change that rule, and after 18 months, we are going to publish for the whole world to see our patent applications even before the patent is granted, which I would label the Steal American Technologies Proposal. Is it still in there?

Mr. Scissors. Well, so—the answer—there is an overarching answer, which is the Congress can always override our trade agreements. There is a clause in all of our trade agreements that this will not infringe on the Congress' ability.

Now, what you are—I think this is still a real issue. If the default changes, if the Congress must do something to change American law to a certain area instead of just do nothing, that has an impact on the U.S.

I think the big issue in data protection is most of our partners in the TPP and around the world don't protect data in exactly the way you are talking about, the way we would like, and the TPP doesn't solve that problem.

Mr. Rohrabacher. Okay.

Mr. Scissors. And I don't want it to set a precedent of not solving the problem going forward.

Mr. Rohrabacher. Okay. Well, let me accept that. But let me also accept that anybody—because I fought—as my colleagues know, I have fought these efforts by multinational U.S. corporations to change the patent law for the last 25 years. And one of the first things, fights, I was in was to make sure American inventors wouldn't have to publish their patent applications until they got their patent issued. And we won that here, and I see no reason for it to be in the TPP whatsoever.

In terms of what we need to do in terms of China and such—and thank you very much for noting that over these years I have actually been very aggressive in talking about predicting what would happen is if we would treat China as if it was any other democratic state.

Japan has a great democracy. They protect people's rights. China doesn't do any of that. But, yet, at times we end up with trade policies and treating China better than we do Japan. How ridiculous is that? And what has it resulted? It has resulted in—because, again, others were making the argument, and thank you for acknowledging that, that if we just really treat China well, they are going to come out and be friendly to us, and they are going to become liberals. I call that the hug-a-Nazi-make-a-liberal theory, which has been disproven over and over again.

So I think that what we are doing now is we have to be very realistic. I think we have a new President that is basically not going to be seen as someone—as a faint-hearted leader. This is not what Donald Trump is going to be. He is going to be a strong leader. He is also going to appreciate friends. It is little simple things like that. And like, if it is not in the interest of the American people specifically, I am not going to do it. These are simple principles but, basically, they are pragmatic moves by a person of principle and of courage as well. So I am actually very optimistic.

I remember when everybody went crazy over this Taiwan phone call. I was saying, they are sending the exact message to Beijing that we want to send them. We are no longer a bunch of pushovers here. We have people—we have a strong leader, and we are going to make sure the world is a safer place, and that the gangsters and dictators of this world better understand that.

And so with that said, one of the other things that has made this a safer world is the hard work of people like you, Mr. Chairman. And we are all very grateful. And I am very pleased now to be the last witness before you take off. We started well over 20 years ago. And I don't know how much longer I am going to be here, I don't know where I am going to be, but I may end up surfing in California, just drinking tequila for the rest of my life, who knows. But the fact is the two of us started out a long time ago, and you have done a great job for our country. And I know this isn't the end of it. This is the end of this phase of that.

So thank you very much. God bless you. There we go.

Mr. SALMON. Well, let me just say that in many ways, this last hearing for me was very cathartic. I kind of started out my China experience as a missionary in 1977 to Taiwan. And I was there for 2 years. I was there when Jimmy Carter severed diplomatic ties with Taiwan, and I remember the reaction of the people there.

I remember my heart being broken at the time, because I grew to love and respect the people of Taiwan so very much. And in the time since then, they have gone from an autocratic regime to a thriving democracy. At the time it was Chiang Kai-shek's son that was the president of Taiwan, and there weren't freely held elections. Since that time, there have been—become one of the more robust democracies in the entire world.

And I was there at the swearing in for Lee Ten-hui, and I remember at the time China lobbying missiles in the Taiwan strait.

With our policy of strategic ambiguity, it was frustrating. It was very, very frustrating. But to be able to have a panel of experts such as yourself sit there and talk about credible, thoughtful solutions to moving forward and making that region of the world a prosperous place and a unified place was very cathartic for me. So I thank you from the bottom of my heart.

This committee hearing was planned long before the infamous phone call over the weekend. But to hear virtually everybody on the panel say it was a good idea, it was a good thing, or it can be a good thing if the policy moves in the right direction, I think is a good message. And I hope that the press corps and this country is picking up on it, because I don't think there are any more talented people in their expertise on China, in fact, probably most are far beneath your realm.

So thank you for your great ideas and your thoughts and your comments, and I greatly appreciate it.

And with that, this committee is now adjourned.

[Whereupon, at 3:30 p.m., the subcommittee was adjourned.]

APPENDIX

MATERIAL SUBMITTED FOR THE RECORD

SUBCOMMITTEE HEARING NOTICE
COMMITTEE ON FOREIGN AFFAIRS
U.S. HOUSE OF REPRESENTATIVES
WASHINGTON, DC 20515-6128

Subcommittee on Asia and the Pacific
Matt Salmon (R-AZ), Chairman

December 6, 2016

TO: MEMBERS OF THE COMMITTEE ON FOREIGN AFFAIRS

You are respectfully requested to attend an OPEN hearing of the Committee on Foreign Affairs, to be held by the Subcommittee on Asia and the Pacific in Room 2172 of the Rayburn House Office Building (and available live on the Committee website at http://www.ForeignAffairs.house.gov):

DATE: Tuesday, December 6, 2016

TIME: 2:00 p.m.

SUBJECT: Step or Stumble: The Obama Administration's Pivot to Asia

WITNESSES: Richard J. Ellings, Ph.D.
                  President
                  The National Bureau of Asian Research

                  Derek M. Scissors, Ph.D.
                  Resident Scholar
                  American Enterprise Institute

                  Ms. Kelley Currie
                  Senior Fellow
                  Project 2049 Institute

                  Mr. Barry C. Lynn
                  Director
                  Open Markets Program
                  New America

By Direction of the Chairman

The Committee on Foreign Affairs seeks to make its facilities accessible to persons with disabilities. If you are in need of special accommodations, please call 202/225-5021 at least four business days in advance of the event, whenever practicable. Questions with regard to special accommodations in general (including availability of Committee materials in alternative formats and assistive listening devices) may be directed to the Committee.

COMMITTEE ON FOREIGN AFFAIRS

MINUTES OF SUBCOMMITTEE ON _____*Asia and the Pacific*_____ HEARING

Day____*Tuesday*____Date_____*12/06/2016*_____Room_____*2172*_____

Starting Time _____*2:00pm*_____Ending Time _____*3:30pm*_____

Recesses |_____| (____to____) (____to____) (____to____) (____to____) (____to____) (____to____)

Presiding Member(s)

Salmon

Check all of the following that apply:

Open Session ☑   Electronically Recorded (taped) ☐
Executive (closed) Session ☐   Stenographic Record ☐
Televised ☐

TITLE OF HEARING:

Step or Stumble: The Obama Administration's Pivot to Asia

SUBCOMMITTEE MEMBERS PRESENT:

Brooks, Perry, Rohrabacher, Chabot
Bera, Gabbard

NON-SUBCOMMITTEE MEMBERS PRESENT: *(Mark with an * if they are not members of full committee.)*

HEARING WITNESSES: Same as meeting notice attached? Yes ☑ No ☐
(If "no", please list below and include title, agency, department, or organization.)

STATEMENTS FOR THE RECORD: *(List any statements submitted for the record.)*

TIME SCHEDULED TO RECONVENE _____
or
TIME ADJOURNED _____*3:30pm*_____

Subcommittee Staff Associate

NBR THE NATIONAL BUREAU of ASIAN RESEARCH

Testimony before the House Committee on Foreign Affairs Subcommittee on Asia and the Pacific

United States House of Representatives

Hearing:

"Step or Stumble: The Obama Administration's Pivot to Asia"

Testimony by:
Richard J. Ellings
President
The National Bureau of Asian Research

December 6, 2016
2172 Rayburn House Office Building

Seattle and Washington, D.C.

1819 L STREET NW, NINTH FLOOR • WASHINGTON, D.C. 20036 USA • PHONE 202 347 9767, FAX 202 347 9766 • NBRDC@NBR.ORG, WWW.NBR.ORG

Chairman Salmon, Ranking member Sherman, distinguished members of the Committee,

It is an honor to share my observations and views with you this afternoon, views that are my own, not those of The National Bureau of Asian Research (NBR). NBR is Senator Henry M. "Scoop" Jackson's dream and legacy, and all of us associated with NBR strive to ensure that that legacy is bipartisan, informed by history and the highest-quality research, and focused on the essential interests of the United States.

The "pivot," better called the rebalance, has been a policy of what might be termed "enhanced more of the same." Let me address the policy first by making two contextual points, and then by assessing recent developments as they relate to the pivot. I will conclude by suggesting some alternative, concrete things that Congress can do in working with the new administration.

First contextual point: Where are we in history? For many reasons this period now appears to be a "hinge moment," as someone wrote recently. It's akin in too many ways to the years immediately preceding World Wars I and II, highlighted by the industrialization and rise of dissatisfied, nationalistic, authoritarian powers. And it differs from these eras in noteworthy ways as well: nuances of the principal rising power, China; the proliferation of nuclear weapons; and America's strategic engagement.

China is the central issue. Today, as this committee's members understand, this continental-sized, dissatisfied, nationalistic, authoritarian power continues to rise, albeit more slowly than it did in the preceding three and a half decades. It continues to industrialize, broaden its services sector, and gain power according to most hard measures. Its industrial sector is at least one and a half times the size of

The National Bureau of Asian Research   *Congressional Testimony*
                                                                                (December 2016)

America's, and in many ways this sector is more integrated vertically as well as horizontally than ours. Often these days we are the assemblers. China has replaced Russia as the number-two military power in the world.

Nonetheless, as China watchers like to point out, the country has all kinds of problems, from environmental degradation and demographic issues to corruption, economic mismanagement, and weak rule of law. Its chief problem is that its unelected leadership is insecure and resorting to tighter control, repressive measures, and nationalistic appeals to bolster its popularity, capitalizing on historical grievances. Correspondingly, its foreign policies have become more aggressive in recent years, far-reaching, and, frankly, farsighted. China has a grand strategy to maximize its wealth, space, and influence and to marginalize its most serious competitors, most notably the United States. Its economic policies have been more, not less, mercantilist in recent years. America's and others' intellectual property (IP) seems to be targeted as much today as ever. Meanwhile, China continues to _not_ help in dealing with Pyongyang, to pursue its extraordinary military modernization, to expand its reach in the South China Sea, and to engage in military harassment of Japan.

Although led by a communist party and driven by extraordinary ambition, and notwithstanding its building bases on islets in the South China Sea, China does not evince a tendency (at least yet) toward direct aggression and conquest of the type witnessed in the mid-twentieth century. It has launched an ambitious set of nationalist, not ideological, programs to bolster its wealth, influence, and prestige globally through the One Belt, One Road initiative, Asian Infrastructure Investment Bank, and Regional Comprehensive Economic Partnership.

But China does pose the challenge of potentially dominating Asia with many values that conflict with those of the post–World War II order. If I were to speculate about what a China-led regional or world order would look like, I would extend what Chinese policies and politics look like today. China would aim to lead a suzerain international system, in which its national leadership would continue to be a melded political, business, and military leadership. A form of China-led mercantilism would count for the international economy, as China shows little evidence of trusting markets for what it deems important products and services such as energy and banking. The resulting system would be fragile because China itself would most likely continue to be led by an insecure, unelected, inherently corrupt elite, and states would not be treated as equals. An insecure Chinese leadership would certainly not tolerate anything close to a peer competitor, especially in Asia. The world would not likely be as prosperous, open, and law-based as it is today. It might be trifurcated into competing North American, European, and Asian centers of power.

For many years, specialists have been predicting political change in China to match its economic achievements. They have been wrong to date, and yet they are right about the future. But we have <u>no</u> ability now to predict <u>when</u> change will actually transpire, or what <u>kind</u> of change. Hope for change cannot be the basis for U.S. policy.

Second contextual point: Viewed from a global, systemic perspective, power is concentrating overwhelmingly in the Asia-Pacific, where all of the world's principal military powers and several of the key middle powers pursue their competing as well as shared national interests. (These countries, in rough descending order of military power, are the United States, China, Russia, India, Japan, South Korea, Pakistan, and North Korea.) Six of these eight powers possess nuclear weapons, and the other two are near nuclear. One, the United States, can project conventional power globally. One, China, is seeking that capability, at least regionally. I characterize the balance in the region as *skewed multipolarity*. It is skewed in part because China has pursued a one-sided arms build-up. For example, whereas China's military budget has increased twelvefold in the past 27 years, Japan's is virtually unchanged in this period.

The National Bureau of Asian Research   *Congressional Testimony*
                                                                    (December 2016)

Given the uneven dispersion of power, the extraordinary pace of change in the balance of power, changes in the domestic affairs of key countries, and increasing questions about U.S. leadership that are voiced in the region, *ambiguity* also describes today's strategic environment. Ambiguity is not good. When nations have a difficult time understanding their strategic environments, many feel insecure and look to expand their allies and defenses; some nations see opportunities to pursue ambitions. China and Russia have been perceiving opportunities, and acting accordingly, to expand their influence and undermine and even replace global and regional institutions—Russia by outright conquest, China by somewhat more subtle and certainly cleverer means.

Today's remarkable economic interdependence, reminding one of pre–World War I conditions, cannot obscure these salient realities. In times like ours, nations are more prone to making calculations that lead to conflict. There is less margin for error by policymakers. Our capacities to remain strong and committed, to assess our competitors, and to form and sustain effective coalitions will be key tests of our leadership.

A quick assessment of the pivot: Multiple administrations have pursued a fairly consistent set of U.S. policies that have sustained general peace and made for an economic miracle in the region, but they have not been adjusted to address the tremendous challenges gathering. While terribly named, the pivot is, in fact, an old and exceedingly helpful concept. The intention to place greater policy focus on the Asia-Pacific goes back decades to the Clinton administration and was emphasized at the outset of President George W. Bush's first term, which aimed primarily at bolstering relationships with allies and friends combined with regional trade liberalization.

President Barack Obama aimed more broadly in the high-profile "pivot" in fall 2011, to strengthen our alliances and friendships, further engage China, bolster regional multilateral institutions, expand trade and investment, strengthen our military presence, end North Korea's nuclear program, and advance democracy and human rights—all to enhance peace, prosperity, and democracy in the region. However, notwithstanding a top State Department official's recent statement that "we are handing the next administration a success story in Asia," the pivot and its predecessor policies on balance have failed to prepare us for the challenges of today, let alone tomorrow.

a) We have not been operating from strategic assessments of our core, defendable interests in the world and of the directions in which key players are moving. We have failed again and again to understand and anticipate Russian intentions and policy, North Korean intentions and policy, and most importantly Chinese intentions and policy. I see no evidence that we have undertaken a serious assessment of the kinds of coalitions that we may face should international tensions rise further and polarization take place. Have we contemplated facing some type of Sino-Russian or Sino-Russian-North Korean-Pakistani coalition if, for example, hostilities were to break out on the Korean Peninsula, in the Taiwan Strait, or in the Sea of Japan? I see no peacetime U.S. strategy built on a tough-minded global assessment—a strategy that, if pursued, might reduce the chances of our facing such coalitions and help contain any hostilities to the commons.

b) In fact, we do not have a military strategy for the Asia-Pacific. We have not decided how to respond to China's "gray aggression," island building in the South China Sea or harassment of the Senkaku Islands by Chinese government-directed fishing boats and the Chinese Coast Guard. We have not decided what is essential to us or what winning would be for various contingencies. Is the effective control of the South China Sea by China crossing a red line or not? Have we adequately prepared, should war be thrust upon us, for a conventional arms victory fought over the commons? What are the red lines for our responding militarily in the commons?

c) Sequestration and "business as usual" procurement have hampered our efforts to do the serious work needed to deter—and if deterrence fails, be prepared to win—a conflict in the region.

d) Indeed, China and North Korea pose expansive and far greater, not smaller, challenges to the United States and its allies than before the pivot. To deter or defeat Chinese forces currently, we are being forced to position our forces farther and farther off the Chinese coastline. We have failed to prevent North Korea from achieving nuclear breakout.

e) We continue to treat trade with China as normal, when what we are facing is a strategic-industrial Chinese policy of extraordinary scope and impact, including impeding our ability to capitalize on our innovations and to innovate in the first place.

f) U.S. companies are increasingly twisted into pretzels trying to operate in China and to access a market that is now about the size of America's. Companies remain under pressure to avoid getting on the bad side of the regime; they try to protect their IP unsuccessfully; and they compete with increasingly strong local companies that are favored in myriad ways. The situation for our companies is tougher, not better.

g) The hoped-for political liberalization of China has not developed from its accession to the World Trade Organization (WTO) or from the world otherwise engaging China. In fact, by most measures the regime is less liberal today than at any time since it joined the WTO.

h) Our leadership in the region is also weaker due to the apparent demise of the Trans-Pacific Partnership (TPP). According to a smug *China Daily* article published days ago, with regard to trade "China is happy to write the rules with all its partners," meaning China's partners in its Regional Comprehensive Economic Partnership initiative.

i) Any further faltering of our commitment to "rebalancing" would jeopardize, just to name one important example, our growing strategic relationship with India.

j) Regarding China's domestic situation, we have not responded substantively to Xi Jinping's so-called anti-corruption campaign and other polices creating the most repressive conditions in China in decades. We have not reacted substantively to China's increasingly bold moves to silence critics outside its borders, including its kidnapping, coercion, and trying of foreign nationals. Our passivity risks conveying the impression that we no longer believe that we hold the moral high ground or care about human rights, or, worse, that we are now intimidated by China's wealth and power.

Given this assessment of current policy, you might not be surprised that I think that we ought to do some things differently. In my view, time is of the essence. We do not have the luxury now of letting our own politics extend beyond the water's edge, nor pursuing a strategy that is "enhanced more of the same."

a) Truly rebalance. End using the term "pivot," but indeed pay more attention to the Asia-Pacific because the region is where power is concentrated, the threat of really big war looms largest, and the global economy is now centered. I'm fine with calling it the Asia-Indo-Pacific, but I don't because it's awkward to say.

b) End sequestration and require a reassessment of U.S. strategic interests, challenges, and opportunities globally and for the Asia-Pacific.

c) Once we complete our assessment of the international strategic environment, we need to decide on core interests and goals consonant with U.S. power. It would be preferable, it seems to me, to be prepared to win unambiguously and with our allies a conventional fight in the commons (thus enhancing deterrence) as opposed to having only the capacity to win a war requiring less credible, direct strikes on China, which risk reciprocal strikes against the U.S. homeland, strikes that could turn nuclear quickly.

d) Accordingly, we need to make some fundamental decisions about how we will counter China's rapidly evolving capabilities and the challenges they present to U.S. assured access. Decisions about strategies and concepts of operation will be necessary if we are to make sensible decisions about R&D and procurement, among other issues. It is urgent that we decide what we need: Do we need more nuclear submarines, new long-range bombers, new generations of cruise missiles, or larger numbers of unmanned aerial vehicles and unmanned underwater vehicles?

e) Pay considerable attention to our allies and friends, including India, and not just verbally or during your and the administration's personal visits to Asia. Without fanfare rebuild our credibility with meaningful investments, coordination, and firm actions. Verbal humiliation is less effective than strong policy.

f) Burden-sharing is imbedded into our close alliance relationships in Asia. As part of our reassessment of the strategic environment and the requirements that emerge from that assessment, cost items for further support from our allies should be identified and negotiated prudently.

g) China's interests today include supporting North Korea as a buffer, as a serious distraction for us requiring our significant attention and resources, and as a potential front if hostilities break out between China and the United States. Terminal High Altitude Area Defense (THAAD) and other deployments that we deem strategically imperative must go forward. With an appropriate level of deployments, China may recalculate its support of a nuclear North Korea.

h) A word about Taiwan. In a nutshell, a congratulatory call from the democratically elected president of Taiwan to the U.S. president-elect may not fit the habit of past presidents-elect, but in the context of the latest, heightened military intimidation of Taiwan by the PRC, it seems justified and strategically grounded.

i) Relaunch the TPP or a substitute as soon as possible so that the United States regains the high ground in regional leadership.

j) At the same time, Congress needs to ensure that the TPP or its substitute allows for national punitive responses to international IP theft and against predatory foreign industrial policies.

k) Treat China in a truthful and business-like manner. The president needs to utilize the powers granted in Section 1637 of the 2015 National Defense Authorization Act to retaliate against foreign entities that steal American IP, including Chinese entities, and to report to Congress on the issue as this law requires. My hunch is that the scale of IP theft will decline sharply as we ratchet up a firm response.

l) The Committee on Foreign Investment in the United States needs beefing up and standards revised. The tangled web of Chinese strategic policies and companies poses a large and complex set of business and national security challenges.

m) Human rights policies underscore our claim to moral leadership. For this reason, and as an antidote to the anti-U.S., anti-Japan, and anti-Western propaganda coming out of Beijing incessantly, I would urge chronicling meticulously and publicizing methodically human rights violations, including international kidnappings, and their political origins. We need policies that make clear and unapologetically the superiority of freedom-loving nations based upon rule of law and limited, democratic government.

In summary, there is no acceptable alternative to U.S. leadership in the Asia-Pacific. No less than in Europe, we cannot allow one country, let alone a dissatisfied, nationalistic, authoritarian one, to dominate the region. That doesn't mean war is inevitable. To the contrary, a peaceful order in the Asia-Pacific that protects core U.S. interests and values is sustainable, but it will require our commitment, new strategies, and exceedingly deft and intelligent leadership. While this is not an exact repeat of the 20th century, the stakes are global and vital. Our country's failure at the center of world power is not an option.

Materials Submitted for the Record by Barry C. Lynn

A Glitch in the Matrix: Why the pivot to Asia has no clothes – *Foreign Policy* -
http://docs.house.gov/meetings/FA/FA05/20161206/105445/HHRG-114-FA05-Wstate-LynnB-20161206-SD001.pdf

Built to Break: The International System of Bottlenecks in the New Era of Monopoly -
Challenge - http://docs.house.gov/meetings/FA/FA05/20161206/105445/HHRG-114-FA05-Wstate-LynnB-20161206-SD002.pdf

Strong and Weak Points in the Supply Chain – Powerpoint Slide -
http://docs.house.gov/meetings/FA/FA05/20161206/105445/HHRG-114-FA05-Wstate-LynnB-20161206-SD003.pdf

How Detroit Went Bottom –Up – *Prospect.org* -
http://docs.house.gov/meetings/FA/FA05/20161206/105445/HHRG-114-FA05-Wstate-LynnB-20161206-SD004.pdf

THE NEW CHINA SYNDROME: American business meets its new master – *Harper's* -
http://docs.house.gov/meetings/FA/FA05/20161206/105445/HHRG-114-FA05-Wstate-LynnB-20161206-SD005.pdf

War, Trade, and Utopia – *The National Interest* -
http://docs.house.gov/meetings/FA/FA05/20161206/105445/HHRG-114-FA05-Wstate-LynnB-20161206-SD006.pdf

Why China has the upper hand in the South China Sea – *Reuters* -
http://docs.house.gov/meetings/FA/FA05/20161206/105445/HHRG-114-FA05-Wstate-LynnB-20161206-SD007.pdf